THE SYMBOLIC USES OF POLITICS

THE
SYMBOLIC
USES OF POLITICS

Murray Edelman

UNIVERSITY OF ILLINOIS PRESS, URBANA, CHICAGO, AND LONDON

To Bacia

ACKNOWLEDGMENTS

Communities of scholars continue to flourish in the recesses of large universities. One such community at the University of Illinois, including Charles Hagan, Philip Monypenny, Jack Peltason, Austin Ranney, and Gilbert Steiner, provided a stimulating and congenial milieu for many years and was responsible for raising many of the questions this book tries to deal with, though I take sole responsibility for these answers. These same colleagues, along with Joseph Gusfield, David Danelski, Merle Kling, and Denis Sullivan, have critically read parts or all of the manuscript and have been helpful in other ways.

Richard Merelman was a perceptive research assistant and Anice Duncan efficiently supervised the typing of the manuscript.

For providing time to work on this study I am very greatly indebted to the John Simon Guggenheim Memorial Foundation and to the Institute of Labor and Industrial Relations and the Center for Advanced Study at the University of Illinois.

The American Political Science Review has given me permission to reprint chapter 2, which originally was published as an article in that journal.

CONTENTS

CHAPTER 1

Introduction

Politics, like religion, love, and the arts, is a theme that men cannot leave alone: not in their behavior, nor in their talk, nor in their writing of history. In all countries and cultures men dwell on lore about the state: what it is and does and should be. The lore includes much that is vague, yet comes to have a powerful emotional pull. It includes much that is plainly contrary to what we see happen, yet the myth is all the more firmly believed and the more dogmatically passed on to others because men want to believe it and it holds them together. Sometimes politics is not myth or emotional at all, but a cool and successful effort to get money from others or power over them. Perhaps it can be cool and successful for some only because it is also obsessional, mythical, and emotional for some or for all. The symbolic side of politics calls for attention, for men cannot know themselves until they know what they do and what surrounds and nurtures them. Man creates political symbols and they sustain and develop him or warp him.

A man's relationship to the state is complicated. The state benefits and it threatens. Now it is "us" and often it is "them." It is an abstraction, but in its name men are jailed or made rich on oil depletion allowances and defense contracts, or killed in wars. For each individual the political constitution condenses all these things, in all their ambivalence and ambiguity. In doing so it symbolizes the complication that the individual is himself, for man is a political animal. This book examines politics as a symbolic form, but it can do so only by looking at man and politics as reflections of each other.

In their obsession with the state, men are of course obsessed with themselves. If politics is as complicated and ambivalent as the men who create it, it is to be expected that its institutions and forms should take on strong meanings: meanings that men cue and teach each other to expect and that are vital for the acquiescence of the general public in the actions of elites and therefore for social harmony. Political forms thus come to symbolize what large masses of men need to believe about the state to reassure themselves. It is the needs, the hopes, and the anxieties of men that determine the meanings. But political forms also convey goods, services, and power to specific groups of men. There is accordingly no reason to expect that the meanings will be limited to the instrumental functions the political forms serve. The capacity of political forms both to serve as a powerful means of expression for mass publics and to convey benefits to particular groups is a central theme of this book.

The systematic research in political science of the last several decades has repeatedly called attention to wide gulfs between our solemnly taught, common sense assumptions about what political institutions do and what they actually do. The uses for the political system of both the common assumption and of the actual consequences are explored in detail later; but a few examples of the divergence are in point here.

Elections are an especially revealing example, for voting is the only form in which most citizens ever participate directly in government and is also the political behavior that has been most widely and most rigorously studied. School teachers, good government groups like the League of Women Voters, and candidates themselves never tire of repeating that voting gives the people control over their officials and policies, that the citizen who fails to vote should not complain if he gets poor government, and that elections are fundamental to democracy. But, rather paradoxically, the voting behavior studies have shown that issues are a minor determinant of how people cast their ballots, most voters being quite ignorant of what the issues are and of which party stands for what position.[1] We also know from studies of legislative and administrative behavior that neither of these depends primarily upon election outcomes. So what people get does not depend mainly on their votes.

It does not follow that election campaigns are unimportant or serve no purpose. It is rather that the functions they serve are different and more varied than the ones we conventionally assume and teach. They give people a chance to express discontents and enthusiasms, to enjoy a sense of involvement.[2] This is participation in a ritual act, however; only in a minor degree is it participation in policy formation. Like all ritual, whether in primitive or modern societies, elections draw attention to common social ties and to the importance and apparent reasonableness of accepting the public policies that are adopted.[3] Without some such device no polity can survive and retain the support or acquiescence of its members. The key point is, however, that elections could not serve this vital social function if the common belief in direct popular control over governmental policy through elections were to be widely questioned. The insistence of the most involved upon general participation in the rite is both understandable and functional in this light. So is the impression individual voters have of the reasoned basis for their votes. One psychiatrist has written of voting that, "perhaps in no other area, save possibly that of religion, is the average person more convinced of the logical, defensible, and wholly rational nature of his decisions."[4]

[1] Angus Campbell, Philip E. Converse, Warren E. Miller, and Donald E. Stokes, *The American Voter* (New York, 1960), pp. 171–187.

[2] Robert E. Lane, *Political Life* (Glencoe, Ill., 1959), Part III.

[3] Ernst Cassirer, *An Essay on Man* (New York, 1946), p. 105; Susanne K. Langer, *Philosophy in a New Key* (New York, 1942), pp. 134–135.

[4] C. W. Wahl, "The Relation Between Primary and Secondary Identifications: Psychiatry and the Group Sciences," in Eugene Burdick and Arthur J. Brodbeck, *American Voting Behavior* (Glencoe, Ill., 1959), p. 263.

This conclusion raises the question of just how people's values do enter into the decisions of public organs and of the extent to which particular procedures make some groups' values carry more weight than others. This question is explored in the chapters that follow, with particular attention to the uses in public policy formation of myths, rites, and other symbolic forms.

Not only does systematic research suggest that the most cherished forms of popular participation in government are largely symbolic, but also that many of the public programs universally taught and believed to benefit a mass public in fact benefit relatively small groups. We can show that many business regulation and other law enforcement policies confer tangible benefits on the regulated businesses while conveying only symbolic reassurance to their ostensible beneficiaries, the consumers. This topic is discussed in detail in Chapter 2.

Political scientists even more commonly recognize that the common and commonsense notions about the basically mechanical role of administrative agencies and courts in "carrying out" legislative or constitutional policy are gross distortions of the process that actually takes place. It is accordingly useful to look searchingly at every unquestioned or widely taught assumption about how government works, for it is a key characteristic of myth that it is generally unquestioned, widely taught and believed, and that the myth itself has consequences, though not the ones it literally proclaims.

If we are to make a start toward recognizing the symbolic elements in governmental proceedings and the impact of symbolic functions upon elite and mass behavior, it is necessary to consider some general characteristics of symbols and the conditions that explain their appearance and meanings. Fortunately, psychologists, anthropologists, and philosophers have learned a great deal about this subject, and the application of this body of knowledge to government leads to some exciting pathways, some fruitful speculations, and even a few firm conclusions.

Basic to the recognition of symbolic forms in the political process is a distinction between politics as a spectator sport and political activity as utilized by organized groups to get quite specific, tangible benefits for themselves. For most men most of the time politics is a series of pictures in the mind, placed there by television news, newspapers, magazines, and discussions. The pictures create a moving panorama taking place in a world the mass public never quite touches, yet one its members come to fear or cheer, often with passion and sometimes with action. They are told of legislatures passing laws, foreign political figures threatening or offering trade agreements, wars starting and ending, candidates for public office losing or winning, decisions made to spend unimaginable sums of money to go to the moon.

There is, on the other hand, the immediate world in which people make and do things that have directly observable consequences. In these activities men can check their acts and assumptions against the consequences and correct errors. There is feedback. Some men, relatively few, are involved in politics in this direct way.

Politics is for most of us a passing parade of abstract symbols, yet a parade which our experience teaches us to be a benevolent or malevolent force that can be close to omnipotent. Because politics does visibly confer wealth, take life, imprison and free people, and represent a history with strong emotional and ideological associations, its processes become easy objects upon which to displace private emotions, especially strong anxieties and hopes.[5]

But it could not serve as conveyor of these fears and aspirations if it were simply a tool or mechanism which we all had the power and knowledge to manipulate for our own advantage. It is central to its potency as a symbol that it is

[5] Harold D. Lasswell, *Psychopathology and Politics* (New York, 1930), pp. 75–76.

remote, set apart, omnipresent as the ultimate threat or means of succor, yet not susceptible to effective influence through any act we as individuals can perform.

Research in a number of different sciences has pointed to the key function of remoteness as an influence upon symbolic meanings. One element involved here is the distinction between referential and condensation symbols. Every symbol stands for something other than itself, and it also evokes an attitude, a set of impressions, or a pattern of events associated through time, through space, through logic, or through imagination with the symbol. Students of this subject have noticed a fundamental distinction among symbols that groups them into two quite separate types. Referential symbols are economical ways of referring to the objective elements in objects or situations: the elements identified in the same way by different people. Such symbols are useful because they help in logical thinking about the situation and in manipulating it. Industrial accident statistics and cost figures in cost plus contracts are referential political symbols, though they may also be condensation symbols. Condensation symbols evoke the emotions associated with the situation. They condense into one symbolic event, sign, or act patriotic pride, anxieties, remembrances of past glories or humiliations, promises of future greatness: some one of these or all of them.[6]

Where condensation symbols are involved, the constant check of the immediate environment is lacking. A traffic policeman at a busy corner may grow entranced momentarily with himself or his stick as representative of the august majesty of the state and indulge in the luxury of arbitrary power, perhaps by favoring traffic on one street; but the lengthening line of cars in front of him and some irate honking will soon remind him that he must face reality: drivers and a prosaic chief of police. There is no such check on the fantasies and conceptualizing of those who never can

[6] Edward Sapir, "Symbolism," in *Encyclopedia of the Social Sciences* (New York, 1934), pp. 492–495.

test objectively their conviction that the government and their home towns abound in communist spies and dupes and that John Birch symbolizes resistance to the threat. Nor is there the check of reality and feedback upon those to whom Adlai Stevenson or Barry Goldwater or Dwight Eisenhower are symbols of reason, intelligence, and virtue in public policy. Conclusive demonstrations that their heroes' policies may often be futile or misconceived are impossible simply because the link between dramatic political announcements and their impact on people is so long and so tangled. These people may be right or they may be wrong. The point is that there is no necessity, and often no possibility, of continuously checking their convictions against real conditions.

No example can ever be wholly free of either referential or of condensation symbols; but the distinction between the two types of behavior is fundamental in realistic political analysis.

Practically every political act that is controversial or regarded as really important is bound to serve in part as a condensation symbol. It evokes a quiescent or an aroused mass response because it symbolizes a threat or reassurance. Because the meaning of the act in these cases depends only partly or not at all upon its objective consequences, which the mass public cannot know, the meaning can only come from the psychological needs of the respondents; and it can only be known from their responses.

One type of research that supports this view appears in the work of Smith, Bruner, and White,[7] who have explored the tie between personality and opinions. They conclude that political opinions serve three different functions for the personality. One of these, object appraisal, or help in understanding the world, can only be performed by those political opinions that are fairly realistic: opinions which, in our terms, are based upon referential symbols and are constantly checked against the objects to which they refer. An opinion

[7] M. Brewster Smith, J. S. Bruner, and R. W. White, *Opinions and Personality* (New York, 1956).

that the chief function of a party platform is to attract votes and not to forecast public policy would presumably further object appraisal.

Neither of the other functions our political opinions serve need meet the check of reality, however; and in both cases the functions are often best served by ignoring reality. Political opinions sometimes help in social adjustment, and this is the reason men are likely to talk politics with those who agree with them, avoid the subject with those who do not, and sometimes shade or change their opinions to create agreement. Finally, political opinions help "externalize" unresolved inner problems. In a time of depression or anxiety a large group of people may come to believe, for example, that Jewish or Communist or Catholic conspiracies in the government explain their business failures or their inability to realize other ambitions. It is important to notice that opinions developed to promote social adjustment or to project inner tensions will continue to be held and will even be strengthened so long as they really do help in social adjustment or in relieving anxieties, whether or not they are consistent with what is happening in the world.

Controversial political acts remote from the individual's immediate experience and which he cannot influence are highly available objects for such opinions. For much of the mass public, that is, they are bound to become condensation symbols, emotional in impact, calling for conformity to promote social harmony, serving as the focus of psychological tensions. The parade of "news" about political acts reported to us by the mass media and drunk up by the public as drama is the raw material of such symbolization. It has everything: remoteness, the omnipotent state, crises, and détentes. More than that, it has the blurring or absence of any realistic detail that might question or weaken the symbolic meanings we read into it. It is no accident of history or of culture that our newspapers and television present little news, that they overdramatize what they report, and that most citizens have only a foggy knowledge of public affairs though often an intensely felt one. If political acts are to promote social adjustment and are to mean what our inner problems require that they mean, then these acts have to be dramatic in outline and empty of realistic detail. In this sense publishers and broadcast licensees are telling the exact truth when they excuse their poor performance with the plea that they give the public what it wants. It wants symbols and not news.

The governments which most often outrage their citizens or force unwelcome changes in their behavior plainly have the greatest need for reassuring symbols. In this light it is no accident that all totalitarian states involve their populations intensively and almost constantly in discussions of public affairs. Mass meetings, political lectures, discussion groups, organizations for every age and occupational group have been the order of the day in all the fascist and communist dictatorships. The communist Chinese device of public self-criticism as a phase of political discussion is only the ad nauseam extension of this efficient device. It exhausts men's energies in passionate attachments to abstract and remote symbols rather than in private creative work. Such work brings the gratifications that come from planned manipulation of the environment: Veblen's "instinct of workmanship." In doing so it creates a personality resistant to manipulation.[8]

Even without much encouragement by the government, obsessive involvement with verbal accounts of political acts occurs in democracies, too, and it has the same numbing impact upon the critical faculties. It can bring gratifications, looming threats, the appearance of victory and of defeat: in election campaigns and in policy battles elsewhere in the government or in international relations. A dramatic symbolic life among abstractions thereby becomes a substitute gratification for the pleasure of remolding the concrete environment.

Some political activity is quite concrete, of course: the

[8] See the comments on this point of Bruno Bettelheim, *The Informed Heart* (Glencoe, Ill., 1959).

work of the professional politician who uses politics to get jobs and votes; the maneuvers of the businessman who uses it to get profitable contracts or greater latitude in his economic activities; the activity of the local reform group out for better schools, playgrounds, and sewers. But a very small fraction of the population uses politics in this way. For most of the public it is a parade of abstractions, and this is as true of many good government and League of Women Voter types at the center as it is of the extremists well to their right and left.

The Swedish sociologist Ulf Himmelstrand has provided support for the propositions just suggested through some ingeniously designed experiments. He declares that: "non-verbal activity often has the property of bringing the actor directly in touch with things, a property which verbal activity in itself has not. Being directly confronted with the things about which he talks regularly gives the actor an opportunity to benefit from feed-back of unanticipated information regarding the things concerned." [9] He found that "the probability of creative or constructive transformation" increases as interactions among people involve proportionately fewer exchanges of words only (though probably with some necessary minimum) and proportionately more non-verbal interactions.

Himmelstrand classifies certain acts as "symbol acts," defined as "acts which have symbols as their exclusive objects, neglecting largely the objective or conceptual referents of these symbols." This finding is peculiarly applicable to the political behavior just discussed, for symbol acts "consist of various ways of approaching, staying in the vicinity of, entering, or remaining in, a setting where certain verbal statements are regularly pronounced . . . may also consist of an extreme adherence to a certain formulation of a statement or in the aggressive responses with which attempts to modify these formulations are met." [10] This is, of course, precisely

[9] Ulf Himmelstrand, *Social Pressures, Attitudes and Democratic Processes* (Stockholm, 1960), p. 34.
[10] *Ibid.*, p. 43. Kornhauser has reached similar conclusions on the basis

what is involved in the obsessive attachment to political symbols characteristic of much political discussion today.

We may be able to learn something about expressive political symbols from aesthetic theory, for an art form consists of condensation symbols. Its function, like that of the abstract political symbols discussed here, is to serve as a vehicle for expression, both for the artist and for the audience, rather than as an instrument for changing the world. Here again remoteness from immediate experience turns out to be a necessary feature. Many artists have recognized that the expressive power of their works is dependent upon their creating a world set apart from the one in which the audience lives and breathes, so that the spectators may find it easier to engage themselves with the artistic symbols. The proscenium arch in the theatre, the stylized language or form of poetry, the frame and distortions of a painting are some devices for creating a special symbolic universe. In a persuasive preface to his play, *Die Braut von Messina*, Friedrich Schiller recognizes that the chorus in the classical Greek play serves exactly this function and argues that it must be served somehow in every artistic creation.[11] Psychological distance from symbols that evoke perceptions and emotions heightens their potency rather than reducing it. Few principles are more centrally involved in the working of government.

The meanings, however, are not in the symbols. They are in society and therefore in men. Political symbols bring out in concentrated form those particular meanings and emotions which the members of a group create and reinforce in each other. There is nothing about any symbol that requires that it stand for only one thing. Cassirer observes that "it is a

of analysis of mass political behavior rather than through the rigorous experiments Himmelstrand employed. Kornhauser regards concern for remote symbols as a major reason for the emergence of masses susceptible to easy manipulation by elites. See William Kornhauser, *The Politics of Mass Society* (Glencoe, Ill., 1959), pp. 60–65.

[11] For a systematic examination of the artistic requirement of a "semblance" rather than a realistic description or a photographic copying of life, see Susanne Langer, *Feeling and Form* (New York, 1953), pp. 45–103.

common characteristic of all symbolic forms that they are applicable to any object whatsoever."[12]

The point is that every political institution and act evokes and reinforces a particular response in its audiences. Permanent institutions like elections, legislative debate and enactment of laws, and courtroom rituals bring out very nearly the same response among the entire population of spectators. In democratic countries these institutions reinforce beliefs in the reality of citizen participation in government and in the rational basis of governmental decisions, regardless of what is said in the course of the proceedings on particular occasions. Men may dislike a winning candidate, law, or judge's decision, yet be reassured by the *forms* of the election, legislature, and court. They may approve a particular administrative ruling, yet be repelled by what they see as the arbitrary manner in which it was reached and issued.[13] So government not only confers benefits; its forms also placate or arouse spectators.

Political analysis must, then, proceed on two levels simultaneously. It must examine how political actions get some groups the tangible things they want from government and at the same time it must explore what these same actions mean to the mass public and how it is placated or aroused by them. In Himmelstrand's terms, political acts are both instrumental and expressive.

In contrast to institutions, transitory political acts or events in the news commonly mean different things to different groups of spectators, dividing men rather than uniting them. Every event comes to be seen as part of a pattern, though groups with conflicting political interests see the patterns differently. A Presidential proposal to increase the number of justices on the Supreme Court fits for many a pattern of events proving that a president with dictatorial aspirations wants to eliminate all resistance. For many others it fits just as neatly into a preconceived pattern of events proving that

12 Ernst Cassirer, *The Myth of the State* (New Haven, Conn., 1946), p. 41.
13 These effects are analyzed in Chapter 4.

the President is fighting against heavy resistance from vested interests for equitable treatment for the underprivileged.

For the spectators of the political scene every act contributes to a pattern of ongoing events that spells threat or reassurance. This is the basic dichotomy for the mass public. The very fact that the same act which one grouping favors looms ominously for another reinforces each side in its perceptions for it seems to make it all the more clear that the enemy is really there, fighting against the good life or against life itself. One student of symbolism has written: "Every act is at once an acceptance *and* (not *or*) a rejection. . . . Identification is compensatory to division; for, if men were not separate from one another, there would be no need for the rhetorician to stress their unity." [14]

For everyone the political scene is a pastiche of several patterns, but always there are threatening ones. That one man's reassurance is another's threat guarantees that threat will always be present for all men. It may be imminent or it may be a potentiality to brood about, but the threatening trends naturally loom larger than the reassuring ones.

All times are "the times that try men's souls." The age one lives in is always in crisis, and especially so since newspaper reading became common. That the times are critical is conventionally cited by elites and politicians as their justification for unpleasant actions that might be expected to arouse resentment and resistance, and the deep conviction that the age is indeed critical brings wide popular support for peacetime drafts, for injecting cancer-producing matter into the air and food supply, and for austerity welfare budgets.

This analysis suggests the corollary that the particular incidents in the news do not really matter so far as the creation of threat perceptions is concerned. No matter what incidents occur and which of these are reported, they will fit nicely as evidence to support people's preconceived hopes and fears. What matters is remoteness, not content. Thus an actual

[14] Hugh D. Duncan, *Language and Literature in Society* (Chicago, 1953), p. 106.

enemy attack or an earthquake has always given men greater confidence and made them act more effectively, for this is something close and concrete with which to cope. It is reports of feints and omens that bring expressive acts with little instrumental value.

Very likely it is not only the threats of which men are told but the frequent and unremitting succession of crisis and détente in the news that produces political docility. Militant speeches, aggressive feints, the highly publicized discovery of espionage, and brushfire wars are succeeded by placatory speeches, troop withdrawals, agreements in principle, and the highly publicized release of spies. In the domestic news there is a similar ebb and flow of threat for each interest grouping. For the unskilled worker there are frequent shifts in plant layoff plans and in unemployment trends generally, in union strike threats, in promised government social security programs, and in the latest word about the adequacy of his children's education and the incidence of child delinquency. If a man's vicarious experience with events that concern him, as far back as he can remember, consists of emergencies, crises, and hazards followed by temporary periods of relief and hope, followed by new crises, what influence will this have upon his behavior? It may well induce helplessness, confusion, insecurity, and greater susceptibility to manipulation by others.

One complication has so far been understated: that men are ambivalent. While one person's threat is another's reassurance, it is also true that every man does, in greater or lesser degree, share his adversary's view. Living in the same society and witnessing the same political drama, some appreciation of one's opponents' passions must be present in every individual.

In the measure that men are torn in this fashion, their susceptibility to persuasion is all the greater. Ambivalence, long a key concept for psychologists, accordingly has far-reaching implications for political behavior as well.

Some threats come to be shared universally or very nearly so and to foster rigidity rather than manipulability. These are the ones that purport to have the same consequences for the whole nation: the threat issuing from other nations, from inscrutable nature, or from a small group within the nation. Because signs of these dangers are most voraciously and universally sought after, newspaper men have both economic and psychological reasons to play them conspicuously: the latest move of the potential foreign foe, or, in another time, the latest depression news. The very language in which developments such as these are discussed makes it difficult to react to them except as threats. "USSR" and "Khrushchev" can come to stand so repeatedly for danger that adaptive thinking becomes unlikely, and political actions that accept the USSR or Khrushchev as reasonable or as potential associates are met with hostility. Thus can the subtle connotations of language freeze perception and conception, a point on which studies in semantics and in psychology come to a common conclusion.[15]

American and Soviet diplomats and analysts, working with each other and with hard facts and discovering bases for agreement in the cold war, may thus be hampered by a rigid consensus of the uninvolved from going very far with negotiation. Neither Khrushchev nor Johnson could do so without the risk of offending groups with wide support.

Political acts, speeches, and gestures involve mass audiences emotionally in politics while rendering them acquiescent to policy shifts through that very involvement. The permanent legal and political institutions reassure people and make of them a supporting bulwark, even while they respond to particular developments with fear or hope.

The complement to this adaptive and acquiescent behavior on the part of spectators is cognitive and rational planning on the part of groups directly involved in maneuvering for tangible values. Utilizing referential symbols, bringing to bear what sanctions they can in the form of organization, money, boycotts, and other deprivations of opposing groups or of gov-

[15] The pathic effects of language upon political identifications are analyzed in Chapter 6.

ernmental authorities, they get what they can. If such forms as voting and legislation, those we herald as bastions of democracy, bring largely ritual, vicarious, and ephemeral mass participation, there remains in America the possibility of real influence for anyone through involvement in the groups that get benefits through playing the administration and bargaining game. Needless to say, possibility is not always reality, and symbolic participation is our lot much of the time. It occurs partly through our own choice, in a sense, but more importantly through the multifaceted symbolism of political acts and institutions.

Two symbolic forms that permeate our political institutions are rite and myth. Both of these are commonly associated with studies of primitive tribes, and anthropologists have taught us a good deal about their dynamics, as has psychoanalytic theory. Much that anthropologists and psychologists say about them has its application in political analysis, not simply as interesting analogy, but as a necessary tool for explanation and prediction.

To study the working of ritual and myth in this area is to examine persisting political institutions, in contrast to the passing parade of news. For rite and myth are persistent, in precisely the same sense and for the same reasons that elections, discussions of politics, patriotic holiday ceremonies, legislative postures, judicial dramas of combat, and administrative busyness are persistent.

Ritual is motor activity that involves its participants symbolically in a common enterprise, calling their attention to their relatedness and joint interests in a compelling way. It thereby both promotes conformity and evokes satisfaction and joy in conformity. Men instinctively try to find meaning and order when placed in a confusing or ambiguous situation. In dances and other motor activity in which primitive man celebrates seasonal changes, the basic order of the universe underlying the "blooming buzzing confusion" of sensations is reaffirmed and the individual reminded of the need to conform to a basic order himself. In rain dances and victory dances men achieve symbolically something they collectively need or want by reaffirming their common interest, denying their doubts, and acting out the result they seek. The motor activity, performed together with others, reassures everyone that there are no dissenters and brings pride and satisfaction in a collective enterprise. A simplified model or semblance of reality is created, and facts that do not fit are screened out of it. Conformity and satisfaction with the basic order are the keynotes; and the acting out of what is to be believed is a psychologically effective mode of instilling conviction and fixing patterns of future behavior.[16]

To quiet resentments and doubts about particular political acts, reaffirm belief in the fundamental rationality and democratic character of the system, and thus fix conforming habits of future behavior is demonstrably a key function of our persisting political institutions: elections, political discussions, legislatures, courts, and administration. Each of them involves motor activity (in which the mass public participates or which it observes from a distance) that reinforces the impression of a political system designed to translate individual wants into public policy. We explain and predict the behavior of participants and spectators only on the assumption that this impression will consistently be fostered in ambiguous acts and language which compel mass attention and mass response and thereby screen out of attention and emotional response the prevalent bargaining among elites.

The political rituals in which masses directly take part are of particular significance in this connection. Most apparent are patriotic ceremonies affirming the greatness, heroism, and nobility of the nation and the pettiness of doubts about the actions it undertakes. More compelling because more subtle is the ritual of election campaigns and political discussion. Most such discussion and most campaign speeches consist of the exchange of cliches among people who agree with each

[16] Jacob L. Moreno, *Psychodrama*, Vol. II (New York, 1945), especially Chapter 6.

other. The talk, therefore, serves to dull the critical faculties rather than to arouse them. Participation of this sort in an emotionally compelling act in which each participant underlines its reality and seriousness for every other is the most potent form of political persuasion.

Myth serves the same purpose as rite, each reinforcing the other. Malinowski has remarked that a native learns his people's myths not from stories, but by living within "the social texture of his tribe." [17] In contemporary society as well, certain political beliefs are socially communicated and are unquestioned. The most conspicuous examples in the United States are precisely the ones I have just questioned: the rational character of the voting act, the reality of the controls elections exert over governmental policy directions, the rational and even mechanical character of judicial and administrative enforcement of the laws.

Malinowski notes that myth is used "to account for extraordinary privileges or duties, for great social inequalities, for severe burdens of rank, whether this be very high or very low": in short for "sociological strain." [18] Clearly these are the very bases of potential resentment which our myths about close popular control over political institutions account for and moderate. Without them the inequalities in wealth, in income, and in influence over governmental allocations of resources can be expected to bring restiveness; with them, potential rebellion is displaced by "constitutional" criticism or approval.

This formulation comes close to Kenneth Burke's enlightening comment that the creation and transformation of political constitutions is the ideal dialectic act in the sense that through it human relations are expressed in all their fullness. [19] On the one hand the constitution legitimizes in

17 Bronislaw Malinowski, *Magic, Science, and Religion and Other Essays* (New York, 1948), p. 93.

18 *Ibid.*, pp. 64, 103.

19 See the discussion of Burke and related observations in Duncan, *op. cit.*, p. 98.

morally unquestionable postulates the predatory use of such bargaining weapons as groups possess: due process of law, freedom of expression, freedom of contract, and so on. On the other hand, it fixes as socially unquestionable fact the primacy of law and of a social order run in accordance with a code that perpetuates popular government and the current consensus on values: the rule of law, the power to regulate commerce, the police power, and so on. The constitution thereby becomes the concise and hallowed expression of man's complex and ambivalent attitude toward others: his wish to aggrandize his goods and powers at the expense of others; his fears that he may suffer from powerful positions of others and from their predations; his seeking for an encompassing principle that will introduce stability and predictability into this explosive clash of interests.

It will shock many to suggest that political constitutions are so largely irrational, in genesis and in impact. The shock itself is pertinent to the observation, for, as one psychiatrist has pointed out, most men are convinced that their political decisions are logical, defensible, and wholly rational, even though "The collectivity of psychotherapeutic experience suggests that the areas of politics and religion are for most of us more deeply immune to the rational processes than are any other portions of our conscious beliefs and value systems." [20]

The key theses of this book bring into open scrutiny the evidence for a truth often vaguely sensed and expressed: that the most conspicuously "democratic" institutions are largely symbolic and expressive in function. But they also make it clear that the notion of evaluating a political system as an instrument which more or less accurately gives individuals what they "want" is much too simple. The very question of what man *is*, let alone what he wants, is in part a product of the political system, and in turn conditions the system. The nature of man and the functioning of the system are part of a single transaction. The expressive and symbolic func-

[20] Wahl, *op. cit.*, p. 263.

tions of the polity are therefore central: not simply a blind for oligarchic rules, though they may sometimes be that, too.

If the conventional study of politics concentrates on how people get the things they want through government, this book concentrates on the mechanisms through which politics influences what they want, what they fear, what they regard as possible, and even who they are.

There is no implication here that elites consciously mold political myths and rituals to serve their ends. Attempts at such manipulation usually become known for what they are and fail. What we find is social role taking, not deception. Potent condensation symbols, as already noted, are created through living "within the social texture"; this is notably true of political forms which become symbols.

To observe politics is to see public officials and candidates acquire and lose followings and to see groups win or fail to win the benefits they claim through government. Using the literature based upon such observations as its data and social, psychological, and linguistic theory as its conceptual framework, this book tries to discover the symbolic processes that tie officials to their followings and that underlie political claims, political quiescence, and the winning of benefits. It finds the major keys to the symbolic potency of governmental acts in everyday public and private activities and not in the manifestly exotic or ceremonial acts of state.

The book therefore explores the *meanings* for large publics of the acts and gestures of leaders, of the settings in which political acts occur, of the language styles and the phrases that permeate political discussion and action, of law enforcement activities. It assumes that what these things mean can be learned from the way people respond to them and from what they do about them. The book also examines the symbolic ties of smaller, organized groups to public officials, and it considers how the responses of the mass of political spectators influence the ability of the organized to win tangible benefits through government.

It tries to highlight the interplay in politics among acts,

actors, settings, language, and masses, and is accordingly divided into sections with these headings. In each section there is occasion to notice the bearing of the other elements upon the one being scrutinized.

By looking for people's differing reactions to political actions, to language forms and terms, to settings, and to leadership styles, the interweaving levels at which politics has consequences can be recognized.

There is no one "real" political system. To people in diverse situations one or another facet is real, for the time being and for the issues that concern them. To define the system, all these perspectives must be taken into account.

CHAPTER 2

Symbols and Political Quiescence

Few explanations of political phenomena are more common than the assertion that the success of some group was facilitated by the "apathy" of other groups with opposing interests. If apathy is not observable in a political context because it connotes an individual's mental state, quiescence is observable. This chapter specifies some conditions associated with political quiescence in the formation of business regulation policies. Although the same general conditions are apparently applicable to the formation of public policies in any area, the argument and the examples used here focus upon the field of government regulation of business in order to permit more intensive treatment.

Political quiescence toward a policy area can be assumed to be a function either of lack of interest or of the satisfaction of whatever interest the quiescent group may have in the policy in question. Our concern here is with the forms of satisfaction. In analyzing the various means by which it can come to pass, the following discussion distinguishes between interests in resources (whether goods or freedoms to act) and interests in symbols connoting the suppression of threats to the group in question.

Three related hypotheses will be considered:

(1) The interests of organized groups in tangible resources or in substantive power are less easily satiable than are interests in symbolic reassurance.

(2) Conditions associated with the occurrence of an interest in symbolic reassurance are:

(a) the existence of economic conditions threatening the security of a large group;

(b) the absence of organization for the purpose of furthering the common interest of that group.

(3) The pattern of political activity represented by lack of organization, interests in symbolic reassurance, and quiescence is a key element in the ability of organized groups to use political agencies in order to make good their claims on tangible resources and power, thus continuing the threat to the unorganized.

Evidence bearing on these hypotheses is marshaled as follows. First, some widely accepted propositions regarding group claims, quiescence, and techniques for satisfying group interests in governmental regulation of business are summarized. Next, some pertinent experimental and empirical findings of other disciplines are considered. Finally, we explore the possibility of integrating the various findings and applying them to the propositions listed above.

I

If the regulatory process is examined in terms of a divergence between political and legal promises on the one hand and resource allocations and group reactions on the other hand, the largely symbolic character of the entire process becomes apparent. What do the studies of government regulation of business tell us of the role and functions of that amorphous group who are affected by these policies, but who are not organized to pursue their interests? The following generalizations would probably be accepted by most students, perhaps with occasional changes of emphasis:

(1) Tangible resources and benefits are frequently not distributed to unorganized political group interests as promised in regulatory statutes and the propaganda attending their enactment.

This is true of the values held out to (or demanded by) groups which regard themselves as disadvantaged and which presumably anticipate benefits from a regulatory policy. There is virtually unanimous agreement among students of the antitrust laws, the Clayton and Federal Trade Commission acts, the Interstate Commerce acts, the public utility statutes and the right-to-work laws, for example, that through much of the history of their administration these statutes have been ineffective in the sense that many of the values they promised have not in fact been realized. The story has not been uniform, of course; but the general point hardly needs detailed documentation at this late date. Herring,[1] Leiserson,[2] Truman,[3] and Bernstein[4] all conclude that few regulatory policies have been pursued unless they proved acceptable to the regulated groups or served the interests of these groups. Redford,[5] Bernstein,[6] and others have offered a "life cycle" theory of regulatory history, showing a more or less regular pattern of loss of vigor by regulatory agencies. For purposes of the present argument it need not be assumed that this always happens but only that it frequently happens in important cases.[7]

(2) When it does happen, the deprived groups often dis-

[1] E. Pendleton Herring, *Public Administration and the Public Interest* (New York, 1936), p. 213.

[2] Avery Leiserson, *Administrative Regulation: A Study in Representation of Interests* (Chicago, 1942), p. 14.

[3] David Truman, *The Governmental Process* (New York, 1951), Chap. 5.

[4] Marver Bernstein, *Regulating Business by Independent Commissions* (New York, 1955), Chap. 3.

[5] Emmette S. Redford, *Administration of National Economic Control* (New York, 1952), pp. 385–386.

[6] Bernstein, *op. cit.*

[7] In addition to the statements in these analytical treatments of the administrative process, evidence for the proposition that regulatory statutes often fail to have their promised consequences in terms of resource allocation are found in general studies of government regulation of business and in empirical research on particular statutes. As an example of the former see Clair Wilcox, *Public Policies Toward Business* (Chicago, 1955). As examples of the latter see Frederic Meyers, *"Right to Work" in Practice* (New York, 1959); Walton Hamilton and Irene Till, *Antitrust in Action*, TNEC Monograph 16 (Washington, D.C., GPO, 1940).

play little tendency to protest or to assert their awareness of the deprivation.

The fervent display of public wrath, or enthusiasm, in the course of the initial legislative attack on forces seen as threatening "the little man" is a common American spectacle. It is about as predictable as the subsequent lapse of the same fervor. Again, it does not always occur, but it happens often enough to call for thorough explanation. The leading students of regulatory processes have all remarked upon it; but most of these scholars, who ordinarily display a close regard for rigor and full exploration, dismiss this highly significant political behavior rather casually. Thus, Redford declares that, "In the course of time the administrator finds that the initial public drive and congressional sentiment behind his directive has wilted and that political support for change from the existing pattern is lacking." [8]

Although the presumed beneficiaries of regulatory legislation often show little or no concern with its failure to protect them, they are nevertheless assumed to constitute a potential base of political support for the retention of these statutes in the law books. The professional politician is probably quite correct when he acts on the assumption that his advocacy of this regulatory legislation, in principle, is a widely popular move, even though actual resource allocations inconsistent with the promise of the statutes are met with quiescence.

[8] Redford, *op. cit.*, p. 383. Similar explanations appear in Herring, *op. cit.*, p. 227, and Bernstein, *op. cit.*, pp. 82–83. Some writers have briefly suggested more rigorous explanations, consistent with the hypotheses discussed in this paper, though they do not consider the possible role of interests in symbolic reassurance. Thus Truman calls attention to organizational factors, emphasizing the ineffectiveness of interest groups "whose interactions on the basis of the interest are not sufficiently frequent or stabilized to produce an intervening organization and whose multiple memberships, on the same account, are a constant threat to the strength of the claim." Truman, *op. cit.*, p. 441. Multiple group memberships are, of course, characteristic of individuals in all organizations, stable and unstable; and "infrequent interactions" is a phenomenon that itself calls for explanation if a common interest is recognized. Bernstein, *loc. cit.*, refers to the "undramatic nature" of administration and to the assumption that the administrative agency will protect the public.

These responses (support of the statute together with apathy toward failure to allocate resources as the statute promises) define the meanings of the law so far as the presumed beneficiaries are concerned.[9] It is the frequent inconsistency between the two types of response that is puzzling.

(3) The most intensive dissemination of symbols commonly attends the enactment of legislation which is most meaningless in its effects upon resource allocation. In the legislative history of particular regulatory statutes the provisions least significant for resource allocation are most widely publicized and the most significant provisions are least widely publicized.

The statutes listed under Proposition 1 as having promised something substantially different from what was delivered are also the ones which have been most intensively publicized as symbolizing protection of widely shared interests. Trust-busting, "Labor's Magna Carta" (the Clayton Act), protection against price discrimination and deceptive trade practices, protection against excessive public utility charges, tight control of union bureaucracies (or, by other groups, the "slave labor law"), federal income taxation according to "ability to pay," are the terms and symbols widely disseminated to the public as descriptive of much of the leading federal and state regulation of the last seven decades, and they are precisely the descriptions shown by careful students to be most misleading. Nor is it any less misleading if one quotes the exact language of the most widely publicized specific provisions of these laws: Section 1 of the Sherman Act, Sections 6 and 20 of the Clayton Act, or the closed shop, secondary boycott, or emergency strike provisions of Taft-Hartley, for example. In none of these instances would a reading of either the text of the statutory provision or the attendant claims and publicity enable an observer to predict even the direction of future regulatory policy, let alone its precise objectives.

Other features of these statutes also stand as the symbols of

[9] Compare the discussion of meaning in George Herbert Mead, *Mind, Self and Society* (Chicago, 1934), pp. 78–79.

threats stalemated, if not checkmated, by the forces of right and justice. Typically, a preamble (which does not pretend to be more than symbolic, even in legal theory) includes strong assurances that the public or the public interest will be protected, and the most widely publicized regulatory provisions always include other nonoperational standards connoting fairness, balance, or equity.

If one asks, on the other hand, for examples of changes in resource allocations that have been influenced substantially and directly by public policy, it quickly appears that the outstanding examples have been publicized relatively little. One thinks of such legislation as the silver purchase provisions, the court definitions of the word "lawful" in the Clayton Act's labor sections, the procedural provisions of Taft-Hartley and the Railway Labor Act, the severe postwar cuts in grazing service appropriations, and changes in the parity formula requiring that such items as interest, taxes, freight rates, and wages be included as components of the index of prices paid by farmers.

Illuminating descriptions of the operational meaning of statutory mandates are found in Truman's study and in Earl Latham's *The Group Basis of Politics*.[10] Both emphasize the importance of contending groups and organizations in day-to-day decision-making as the dynamic element in policy formation; and both distinguish this element from statutory language as such.[11]

We are only beginning to get some serious studies of the familiarity of voters with current public issues and of the intensity of their feelings about issues; but successful political professionals have evidently long acted on the assumption that there is in fact relatively little familiarity, that expressions of deep concern are rare, that quiescence is common, and that, in general, the congressman can count upon stereo-

[10] Truman, *op. cit.*, pp. 439–446; Earl Latham, *The Group Basis of Politics* (Ithaca, N.Y., 1952), Chap. 1.

[11] I have explored this effect in labor legislation in "Interest Representation and Labor Law Administration," *Labor Law Journal*, Vol. 9 (1958), pp. 218–226.

typed reactions rather than persistent, organized pursuit of material interests on the part of most constituents.[12]

(4) Policies severely denying resources to large numbers of people can be pursued indefinitely without serious controversy.

The silver purchase policy, the farm policy, and a great many other subsidies are obvious examples. The antitrust laws, utility regulations, and other statutes ostensibly intended to protect the small operator or the consumer are less obvious examples, though there is ample evidence, some of it cited below, that these usually support the proposition as well.

The federal income tax law offers a rather neat illustration of the divergence between a widely publicized symbol and actual resource allocation patterns. The historic constitutional struggle leading up to the Sixteenth Amendment, the warm defenses of the principle of ability to pay, and the frequent attacks upon the principle through such widely discussed proposals as that for a 25 per cent limit on rates have made the federal tax law a major symbol of justice. While the fervent rhetoric from both sides turns upon the symbol of a progressive tax and bolsters the assumption that the system is highly progressive, the bite of the law into people's resources depends upon quite other provisions and activities that are little publicized and that often seriously qualify its progressive character. Special tax treatments arise from such devices as family partnerships, gifts inter vivos, income-splitting, multiple trusts, percentage depletion, and deferred compensation.

Tax evasion alone goes far toward making the symbol of "ability to pay" hollow semantically though potent symbolically. While 95 per cent of income from wages and salaries is taxed as provided by law, taxes are actually collected on only 67 per cent of taxable income from interest, divi-

[12] See Lewis A. Dexter, "Candidates Must Make the Issues and Give Them Meaning," *Public Opinion Quarterly*, Vol. 10 (1955–56), pp. 408–414.

dends, and fiduciary investments and on only about 36 per cent of taxable farm income.[13] By and large, the recipients of larger incomes can most easily benefit from exemptions, avoidance, and evasions. This may or may not be desirable public policy, but it certainly marks a disparity between symbol and effect upon resources.

II

These phenomena are significant for the study of the political process for two reasons. First, there is a substantial degree of consistency in the group interest patterns associated with policies on highly diverse subject matters. Second, they suggest that nonrational reaction to symbols among people sharing a common governmental interest is a key element in the process. The disciplines of sociology, social psychology, and semantics have produced some pertinent data on the second point, which will now be investigated.

Harold Lasswell wrote three decades ago that "Politics is the process by which the irrational bases of society are brought out into the open." He marshaled some support in case studies for several propositions that have since been confirmed with richer and more direct experimental evidence. "The rational and dialectical phases of politics," he said, "are subsidiary to the process of redefining an emotional consensus." He argued that "widespread and disturbing changes in the life-situation of many members of society" produce adjustment problems which are resolved largely through symbolization, and he suggested that "Political demands probably bear but a limited relevance to social needs." [14]

The frame of reference suggested by these statements is sometimes accepted by political scientists today when they

[13] Randolph E. Paul, "Erosion of the Tax Base and Rate Structure," in Joint Committee on the Economic Report, *Federal Tax Policy for Economic Growth and Stability*, 84th Congress, 1st Session, 1955, pp. 123–138.

[14] *Psychopathology and Politics* (New York, 1960), pp. 184, 185.

study voting behavior and when they analyze the legislative process. Its bearing on policy formation in the administrative process is not so widely recognized. It is true that cognition and rationality are central to administrative procedures to a degree not true of legislation or voting. But this is not the same thing as saying that administrative policies or administrative politics are necessarily insulated from the "process of redefining an emotional consensus."

Let us consider now some experimental findings and conclusions specifying conditions under which groups or personality types are prone to respond strongly to symbolic appeals and to distort or ignore reality in a fashion that can be politically significant.

(1) People read their own meanings into situations that are unclear or provocative of emotion. As phrased by Fensterheim, "The less well defined the stimulus situation, or the more emotionally laden, the greater will be the contribution of the perceiver." [15] This proposition is no longer doubted by psychologists. It is the justification for so-called projective techniques and is supported by a great deal of experimental evidence.

Now it is precisely in emotionally laden and poorly defined situations that the most widely and loudly publicized public regulatory policies are launched and administered. If, as we have every reason to suppose, there is little cognitive familiarity with issues, the "interest" of most of the public is likely

[15] Herbert Fensterheim, "The Influence of Value Systems on the Perception of People," *Journal of Abnormal and Social Psychology*, Vol. 48 (1953), p. 93. Fensterheim cites the following studies in support of the proposition: D. Krech and R. S. Crutchfield, *Theory and Problems of Social Psychology* (New York, 1948); A. S. Luchins, "An Evaluation of Some Current Criticisms of Gestalt Psychological Work on Perception," *Psychological Review*, Vol. 58 (1951), pp. 69–95; J. S. Bruner, "One Kind of Perception: A Reply to Professor Luchins," *Psychological Review*, Vol. 58 (1951), pp. 306–312; and the chapters by Bruner, Frenkel-Brunswik, and Klein in R. R. Blake and G. V. Ramsey, *Perception: An Approach to Personality* (New York, 1951). See also Charles Osgood, Percy Tannenbaum, and George Suci, *The Measurement of Meaning* (Urbana, Ill., 1957).

to be a function of other sociopsychological factors. What these other factors are is suggested by certain additional findings.

(2) It is characteristic of large numbers of people in our society that they see and think in terms of stereotypes, personalization, and oversimplifications, that they cannot recognize or tolerate ambiguous and complex situations, and that they accordingly respond chiefly to symbols that oversimplify and distort. This form of behavior (together with other characteristics less relevant to the political process) is especially likely to occur where there is insecurity occasioned by failure to adjust to real or perceived problems.[16] Frenkel-Brunswik has noted that "such objective factors as economic conditions" may contribute to the appearance of the syndrome, and hence to its importance as a widespread group phenomenon attending the formulation of public policy.[17] Such behavior is sufficiently persistent and widespread to be politically significant only when there is social reinforcement of faith in the symbol. When insecurity is individual, without communication and reinforcement from others, there is little correlation with ethnocentricity or its characteristics.[18]

A different kind of study suggests the extent to which reality can become irrelevant for persons very strongly committed to an emotion-satisfying symbol. Festinger and his as-

[16] Among the leading general and experimental studies dealing with the phenomenon are: M. Rokeach, "Generalized Mental Rigidity as a Factor in Ethnocentrism," *Journal of Abnormal and Social Psychology*, Vol. 43 (1948), pp. 259–277; R. R. Canning and J. M. Baker, "Effect of the Group on Authoritarian and Non-authoritarian Persons," *American Journal of Sociology*, Vol. 64 (1959), pp. 579–581; A. H. Maslow, "The Authoritarian Character Structure," *Journal of Social Psychology*, Vol. 18 (1943), p. 403; T. W. Adorno and others, *The Authoritarian Personality* (New York, 1950); Gerhart Saenger, *The Psychology of Prejudice* (New York, 1953), pp. 123–138; Erich Fromm, *Escape from Freedom* (New York, 1941); R. K. Merton, *Mass Persuasion* (New York, 1950).

[17] Else Frenkel-Brunswik, "Interaction of Psychological and Sociological Factors in Political Behavior," *The American Political Science Review*, Vol. 46 (1952), pp. 44–65.

[18] Adorno and others, *op. cit.*

sociates, as participant-observers, studied a group of fifteen persons who were persuaded that the world would come to an end on a particular day in 1956 and that they as believers would be carried away in a flying saucer. With few exceptions the participants refused to give up their belief even after the appointed day had passed. The Festinger study concludes that commitment to a belief is likely to be strengthened and reaffirmed in the face of clear disproof of its validity where there is a strong prior commitment (many of the individuals involved had actually given away their worldly goods) and where there is continuing social support of the commitment by others (two members who lost faith lived where they had no further contact with fellow members of the group; those who retained their faith had continued to see each other). What we know of previous messianic movements of this sort supports this hypothesis.[19]

(3) Emotional commitment to a symbol is associated with contentment and quiescence regarding problems that would otherwise arouse concern.

It is a striking fact that this effect has been noticed and stressed by careful observers in a number of disparate fields, using quite different data and methods. Adorno reports it as an important finding in *The Authoritarian Personality*: "Since political and economic events make themselves felt apparently down to the most private and intimate realms of the individual, there is reliance upon stereotype and similar avoidance of reality to alleviate psychologically the feeling of anxiety and uncertainty and provide the individual with the illusion of some kind of intellectual security." [20]

In addition to the support it gets from psychological experiment, the phenomenon has been remarked by scholars in the fields of semantics, organizational theory, and political science. Albert Salomon points out that "Manipulation of social images makes it possible for members of society to be-

[19] Leon Festinger, Henry Riecken, and Stanley Schachter, *When Prophecy Fails* (Minneapolis, 1956).
[20] Adorno and others, *op. cit.*, p. 665.

lieve that they live not in a jungle, but in a well organized and good society." [21] Harold Lasswell put it as follows:

It should not be hastily assumed that because a particular set of controversies passes out of the public mind that the implied problems were solved in any fundamental sense. Quite often a solution is a magical solution which changes nothing in the conditions affecting the tension level of the community, and which merely permits the community to distract its attention to another set of equally irrelevant symbols. The number of statutes which pass the legislature, or the number of decrees which are handed down by the executive, but which change nothing in the permanent practices of society, is a rough index of the role of magic in politics. . . . Political symbolization has its catharsis function . . . . [22]

Chester Barnard, an uncommonly astute analyst of his own long experience as an executive, concluded that "Neither authority nor cooperative disposition . . . will stand much overt division on formal issues in the present stage of human development. Most laws, executive orders, decisions, etc., are in effect formal notice that all is well — there is agreement, authority is not questioned." [23]

Kenneth Burke makes much the same point. Designating political rhetoric as "secular prayer," he declares that its function is "to sharpen up the pointless and blunt the too sharply pointed." [24] Elsewhere, he points out that laws themselves serve this function, alleging that positive law is *itself* "the test of a judgment's judiciousness." [25]

(4) An active demand for increased economic resources or fewer political restrictions on action is not always operative. It is, rather, a function of comparison and contrast with reference groups, usually those not far removed in socioeconomic status.

[21] Albert Salomon, "Symbols and Images in the Constitution of Society," in L. Bryson, L. Finkelstein, H. Hoagland, and R. M. MacIver (eds.), *Symbols and Society* (New York, 1955), p. 110.

[22] Lasswell, *op. cit.*, p. 195.

[23] Chester I. Barnard, *The Functions of the Executive* (Cambridge, Mass., 1938), p. 226.

[24] Kenneth Burke, *A Grammar of Motives* (New York, 1945), p. 393.

[25] *Ibid.*, p. 362.

This is, of course, one of the most firmly established propositions about social dynamics; one that has been supported by macrosociological analysis,[26] by psychological experiment,[27] and by observation of the political process, particularly through contrast between political quiescence and protest or revolutionary activity.[28]

The proposition helps explain failure to demand additional resources where such behavior is socially sanctioned and supported. It also helps explain the insatiability of the demand by some organized groups for additional resources (i.e., the absence of quiescence) where there is competition for such resources among rival organizations and where it is acquisitiveness that is socially supported. This behavior is more fully analyzed in Chapter 8.

(5) The phenomena discussed above (the supplying of meaning in vague situations, stereotypes, oversimplification, political quiescence) are in large measure associated with social, economic, or cultural factors affecting large segments of the population. They acquire political meaning as group phenomena.

Even among the psychologists, some of whom have been notably insensitive to socialization and environment as explanations and phases of the individual traits they identify, there are impressive experimental findings to support the proposition. In analyzing the interview material of his *authoritarian personality* study, Adorno concluded that "our general cultural climate" is basic in political ideology and in stereotyped political thinking, and he catalogued some standardizing aspects of that climate.[29] His finding, quoted above, regarding the relation of symbols to quiescence is also phrased to emphasize its social character. Lindesmith and Strauss

[26] Mead, *op. cit.*; Ernst Cassirer, *An Essay on Man*.

[27] See James G. March and Herbert A. Simon, *Organizations* (New York, 1958), pp. 65–81, and studies cited there.

[28] See, e.g., Murray Edelman, "Causes of Fluctuations in Popular Support for the Italian Communist Party Since 1946," *Journal of Politics*, Vol. 20 (1958), pp. 547–550; Arthur M. Ross, *Trade Union Wage Policy* (Berkeley and Los Angeles, 1948).

[29] Adorno and others, *op. cit.*, p. 655.

make a similar point, emphasizing the association between symbols and the reference groups to which people adhere.[30]

Another type of research has demonstrated that because interests are typically bound up with people's social situation, attitudes are not typically changed by ex parte appeals. The function of propaganda is rather to activate socially rooted interests. One empirical study which arrives at this conclusion sums up the thesis as follows: "Political writers have the task of providing 'rational' men with good and acceptable reasons to dress up the choice which is more effectively determined by underlying social affiliations."[31]

George Herbert Mead makes the fundamental point that symbolization itself has no meaning apart from social activity: "Symbolization constitutes objects . . . which would not exist except for the context of social relationships wherein symbolization occurs."[32]

III

These studies offer a basis for understanding more clearly what it is that different types of groups expect from government and under what circumstances they are likely to be satisfied or restive about what is forthcoming. Two broad patterns of group interest activity vis-à-vis public regulatory policy are evidently identifiable on the basis of these various modes of observing the social scene. The two patterns may be summarized in the following shorthand fashion:

[30] Alfred R. Lindesmith and Anselm L. Strauss, *Social Psychology* (New York, 1956), pp. 253–255. For a report of another psychological experiment demonstrating that attitudes are a function of group norms, see I. Sarnoff, D. Katz, and C. McClintock, "Attitude-Change Procedures and Motivating Patterns," in Daniel Katz and others (eds.), *Public Opinion and Propaganda* (New York, 1954), pp. 308–309; also Festinger, Riecken, and Shachter, *op. cit.*

[31] Paul F. Lazarsfeld, Bernard Berelson, and Hazel Gaudet, *The People's Choice* (New York, 1944), p. 83. For an account of an experiment reaching the same conclusion see S. M. Lipset, "Opinion Formation in a Crisis Situation," *Public Opinion Quarterly*, Vol. 17 (1953), pp. 20–46.

[32] Mead, *op. cit.*, p. 78.

(1) Pattern A: a relatively high degree of organization — rational, cognitive procedures — precise information — an effective interest in specifically identified, tangible resources — a favorably perceived strategic position with respect to reference groups — relatively small numbers.

(2) Pattern B: shared interest in improvement of status through protest activity — an unfavorably perceived strategic position with respect to reference groups — distorted, stereotyped, inexact information and perception — response to symbols connoting suppression of threats — relative ineffectiveness in securing tangible resources through political activity — little organization for purposeful action — quiescence — relatively large numbers.

It is very likely misleading to assume that some of these observations can be regarded as causes or consequences of others. That they often occur together is both a more accurate observation and more significant. It is also evident that each of the patterns is realized in different degrees at different times.

While political scientists and students of organizational theory have gone far toward a sophisticated description and analysis of Pattern A, there is far less agreement and precision in describing and analyzing Pattern B and in explaining how it intermeshes with Pattern A.

The most common explanation of the relative inability of large numbers of people to realize their economic aspirations in public policy is in terms of invisibility. The explanation is usually implicit rather than explicit, but it evidently assumes that public regulatory policy facilitating the exploitation of resources by knowledgeable organized groups (usually the "regulated") at the expense of taxpayers, consumers, or other unorganized groups is possible only because the latter do not know it is happening. What is invisible to them does not arouse interest or political sanctions.

On a superficial level of explanation this assumption is no doubt valid. But it is an example of the danger to the social scientist of failure to inquire transactionally: of assuming, in this instance, (1) that an answer to a questioner, or a questionnaire, about what an individual "knows" of a regulatory policy at any point in time is in any sense equivalent to specification of a group political interest; and (2) that the sum of many individual knowings (or not knowings) as reported to a questioner is a *cause* of effective (or ineffective) organization, rather than a consequence of it, or simply a concomitant phase of the same environment. If one is interested in policy formation, what count are the assumptions of legislators and administrators about the determinants of future political disaffection and political sanctions. Observable political behavior, as well as psychological findings, reveal something of these assumptions.

There is, in fact, persuasive evidence of the reality of a political interest in continuing assurances of protection against economic forces understood as powerful and threatening. The most relevant evidence lies in the continuing utility of old political issues in campaigns. Monopoly and economic concentration, antitrust policy, public utility regulation, banking controls, and curbs on management and labor are themes that party professionals regard as good for votes in one campaign after another, and doubtless with good reason. They know that these are areas in which concern is easily stirred. In evaluating allegations that the public has lost "interest" in these policies the politician has only to ask himself how much apathy would remain if an effort were made formally to repeal the antitrust, public utility, banking, or labor laws. The answers and the point become clear at once.

The laws may be repealed in effect by administrative policy, budgetary starvation, or other little publicized means; but the laws as symbols must stand because they satisfy interests that are very strong indeed: interests that politicians fear will be expressed actively if a large number of voters are led to believe that their shield against a threat has been removed.

More than that, it is largely as symbols of this sort that these statutes have utility to most of the voters. If they function as reassurances that threats in the economic environment are under control, their indirect effect is to permit greater claims upon tangible resources by the organized groups concerned than would be possible if the legal symbols were absent.

To say this is not to assume that everyone objectively affected by a policy is simply quiescent rather than apathetic or even completely unaware of the issue. It is to say that those who are potentially able and willing to apply political sanctions constitute the politically significant group. It is to suggest as well that incumbent or aspiring congressmen are less concerned with individual constituents' familiarity or unfamiliarity with an issue as of any given moment than with the possibility that the interest of a substantial number of them *could* be aroused and organized if he should cast a potentially unpopular vote on a bill or if a change in their economic situation should occur. The shrewder and more effective politicians probably appreciate intuitively the validity of the psychological finding noted earlier: that where public understanding is vague and information rare, interests in reassurance will be all the more potent and all the more susceptible to manipulation by political symbols.

We have already noted that it is one of the demonstrable functions of symbolization that it induces a feeling of well-being: the resolution of tension. Not only is this a major function of widely publicized regulatory statutes, but it is also a major function of their administration. Some of the most widely publicized administrative activities can most confidently be expected to convey a sense of well-being to the onlooker because they suggest vigorous activity while in fact signifying inactivity or protection of the "regulated."

One form this phenomenon takes is noisy attacks on trivia. The Federal Trade Commission, for example, has long been noted for its hit-and-miss attacks on many relatively small firms involved in deceptive advertising or unfair trade practices while it continues to overlook much of the really significant activity it is ostensibly established to regulate: monopoly, interlocking directorates, and so on.[33]

Another form it takes is prolonged, repeated, well-publicized attention to a significant problem which is never solved. A notable example is the approach of the Federal Communications Commission to surveillance of program content in general and to discussions of public issues on the air in particular. In the postwar period we have had the Blue Book, the Mayflower Policy, the abolition of the Mayflower Policy, and the announcement of a substitute policy; but the radio or television licensee is in practice perfectly free, as he has been all along, to editorialize, with or without opportunity for opposing views to be heard, or to avoid serious discussion of public affairs entirely.

The most obvious kinds of dissemination of symbolic satisfactions are to be found in administrative dicta accompanying decisions and orders, in press releases, and in annual reports. It is not uncommon to give the rhetoric to one side and the decision to the other. Nowhere does the FCC wax so emphatic in emphasizing public service responsibility, for example, as in decisions permitting greater concentration of control in an area, condoning license transfers at inflated prices, refusing to impose sanctions for flagrantly sacrificing program quality to profits, and so on.[34]

The integral connection is apparent between symbolic satisfaction of the disorganized, on the one hand, and the success of the organized, on the other, in using governmental instrumentalities as aids in securing the tangible resources they claim.

Public policy may usefully be understood as the resultant of the interplay among groups.[35] But the political and socio-

[33] Cf. Wilcox, *op. cit.*, pp. 281, 252–255.

[34] Many examples may be found in the writer's study entitled *The Licensing of Radio Services in the United States, 1927 to 1947* (Urbana, Ill., 1950).

[35] For discussions of the utility of this view to social scientists, see Arthur F. Bentley, *The Process of Government* (1908; New York, reprint 1949); Truman, *op. cit.*

psychological processes discussed here mean that groups which present claims upon resources may be rendered quiescent by their success in securing nontangible values. Far from representing an obstacle to organized producers and sellers, they become defenders of the very system of law which permits the organized to pursue their interests effectively.

Thurman Arnold has pointed out how the antitrust laws perform precisely this function:

The actual result of the antitrust laws was to promote the growth of great industrial organizations by deflecting the attack on them into purely moral and ceremonial channels . . . every scheme for direct control broke to pieces on the great protective rock of the antitrust laws. . . .

The antitrust laws remained as a most important symbol. Whenever anyone demanded practical regulation, they formed an effective moral obstacle, since all the liberals would answer with a demand that the antitrust laws be enforced. Men like Senator Borah founded political careers on the continuance of such crusades, which were entirely futile but enormously picturesque, and which paid big dividends in terms of personal prestige.[36]

Arnold's subsequent career as chief of the antitrust division of the Department of Justice did as much to prove his point as his writings. For a five-year period he instilled unprecedented vigor into the division, and his efforts were widely publicized. He thereby unquestionably made the laws a more important symbol of the protection of the public; but despite his impressive intentions and talents, monopoly, concentration of capital, and restraint of trade were not seriously threatened or affected.

This is not to suggest that signs or symbols in themselves have any magical force as narcotics. They are, rather, the only means by which groups not in a position to analyze a complex situation rationally may adjust themselves to it, through stereotypization, oversimplification, and reassurance.

[36] *The Folklore of Capitalism* (New Haven, Conn., 1937), pp. 212, 215, 216.

There have, of course, been many instances of effective administration and enforcement of regulatory statutes. In each such instance it will be found that organized groups have had an informed interest in effective administration. Sometimes the existence of these groups is explicable as a holdover from the campaign for legislative enactment of the basic statute; and often the initial administrative appointees are informed, dedicated adherents of these interests. They are thus in a position to secure pertinent data and to act strategically, helping furnish "organization" to the groups they represent. Sometimes the resources involved are such that there is organization on both sides; or the more effective organization may be on the "reform" side. The securities exchange legislation is an illuminating example, for after Richard Whitney's conviction for embezzlement, key officials of the New York Stock Exchange recognized their own interest in supporting controls over less scrupulous elements. This interest configuration doubtless explains the relative popularity of the SEC in the thirties both with regulated groups and with organized liberal groups.

IV

The evidence considered here suggests that we can make an encouraging start toward defining the conditions in which myth and symbolic reassurance become key elements in the governmental process. The conditions[37] are present in substantial degree in many policy areas other than business regulation. They may well be maximal in the foreign policy area, and a similar approach to the study of foreign policy formation would doubtless be revealing.

Because the requisite conditions are always present in some degree, every instance of policy formulation involves a "mix" of symbolic effect and rational reflection of interests in resources, though one or the other may be dominant in

[37] They are listed above under "Pattern B."

41

any particular case. One type of mix is exemplified by such governmental programs outside the business regulation field as public education and social security. There can be no doubt that these programs do confer important tangible benefits upon a very wide public, very much as they promise to do. They do so for the reasons suggested earlier. Business organizations, labor organizations, teachers' organizations, and other organized groups benefit from these programs and have historically served to focus public attention upon the resources to be gained or lost. Their task has been all the easier because the techniques for achieving the benefits are fairly readily recognizable.

But the financing of these same programs involves public policies of a different order. Here the symbol of "free" education and other benefits, the complexity of the revenue and administrative structure, and the absence of organization have facilitated the emergence of highly regressive payroll, property, and head taxes as the major sources of revenue. Thus, business organizations, which by and large support the public schools that provide their trained personnel and the social security programs that minimize the costs of industrial pensions, pay relatively little for these services, while the direct beneficiaries of the "free" programs pay a relatively high proportion of the costs. Careful analysis of the "mix" in particular programs should prove illuminating.

If the conditions facilitating symbolic reassurance are correctly specified, there is reason to question some common assumptions about strategic variables in policy formulation and reason also to devise some more imaginative models in designing research in this area. The theory discussed here suggests, for example, a tie between the emergence of conditions promoting interests in symbolic reassurance and widened freedom of policy maneuver for the organized. It implies that the number of adherents of a political interest may have more to do with whether the political benefit offered is tangible or symbolic than with the quantity or quality of tangible resources allocated. It suggests that the factors that explain voting behavior can be quite different from the factors that explain resource allocations through government. The fact that large numbers of people are objectively affected by a governmental program may actually serve in some contexts to weaken their capacity to exert a political claim upon tangible values.

A number of recent writers, to take another example, have suggested that it is the "independence" of the independent regulatory commissions which chiefly accounts for their tendency to become tools of the groups they regulate. The hypotheses suggested here apply to regulatory programs administered in cabinet departments as well; and their operation is discernible in some of these programs when the specified conditions are present. The grazing service and the antitrust division are examples.

In terms of research design, the implications of the analysis probably lie chiefly in the direction of emphasizing an integral tie of political behavior to underlying and extensive social interaction. Analysts of political dynamics must have a theory of relevance; but the directly relevant may run farther afield than has sometimes been assumed. Political activities of all kinds require the most exhaustive scrutiny to ascertain whether their chief function is symbolic or substantive. The "what" of Lasswell's famous definition of politics is a complex universe in itself.

CHAPTER 3

The Administrative System as Symbol

I

To control automobile speeding within a 65-mile-an-hour limit or to enforce a $1.15 minimum wage provision are concrete administrative objectives. In these and similar cases the administrator's problem is to maximize compliance and cooperation, for there will always be resistance, footdragging, and some overt defiance. If there were no resistance, there would be no need for the administrative program at all; and if it were impossible to increase the frequency of compliance through governmental action, there would equally obviously be no reason for administrative action.

Both the supporters and the defiers will, however, be clear as to what they are supporting or defying. They will talk and act with respect to the same concrete issue, and they can rationally choose behaviors which will further their objectives (though probably not in optimal fashion). In this kind of situation an administrator will try to achieve a satisfactory degree of compliance by increasing the material, moral, sunk, or other costs of defiance or by rewarding compliance.[1]

Concrete legal objectives are ordinarily pursued as though administrators and potential defiers were involved in a game

[1] Herbert A. Simon, Donald W. Smithburg, and Victor A. Thompson, *Public Administration* (New York, 1950), Chaps. 21, 22.

with rather clear rules. The basic rule is that a fairly large proportion of the instances of noncompliance will not be detected or penalized. Automobile drivers and policemen are both aware that most speeders will not be caught or fined, and both adapt their behavior to this assumption: drivers speed when the chance of being caught is slight or considered worth taking. Policemen stop some but not all violators, and let some of these off with a warning. As long as the game is played in this way, both drivers and policemen accept the order of things fairly contentedly: drivers paying occasional fines complainingly but without massive political protest, policemen noticing a certain amount of modest surpassing of the posted limits without further action. Similarly, employers accept health, safety, child labor, and minimum wage laws on the assumption that inspectors will appear at the plant only once in a while, and that if they are caught in violations on *these* occasions, a fine may have to be paid. The game of taking calculated risks in filing income tax returns is so clearly understood and so universally played that it needs only to be mentioned here.

Fortunately for scholarship and for "constitutional" government, we get just enough administrators ignorant of this rule of the game to serve as an object lesson in the disaster that its violation brings and in the wholly new symbolic relationship that then occurs. Officer Muller of the Chicago police force dismayed and pained his superiors some years ago by systematically ticketing every good citizen who took advantage of the long-standing practice of parking in a no-parking zone near City Hall. After high state and city officials had received this treatment, the conscientious Mr. Muller was assigned to a remote beat. It was never assumed by either the Police Department or the public that enjoyed the story in the newspapers that such substitution of ordinances for the game could be allowed to continue. Similarly, national and local automobile organizations protest and citizens grow righteously irate when a village creates a speed trap and really penalizes every violator. Victor Thompson has described in detail and with rare political insight the battle that occurred inside the World War II OPA Rationing Division between some lawyers determined to read legal language literally and catch every chiseler and the administrators determined to play the only game that would permit OPA to survive.[2]

Each legal offense or administrative enforcement program is a separate game with its own stakes, penalties, and ploys, and these very enormously from one such game to another. Not the size of the stakes or the penalties, but rather the meaning of the offense to enforcers and possible violators is what determines whether a game or a dogma is involved. Even murder falls into the game class in our society, though as a kind of limiting case. Here the stakes and the penalties are high; but the rules prescribe many avenues for avoiding detection and even more for avoiding conviction if detected. If we really regarded murder as an unacceptable and unforgivable act, as we pretend to do, we would certainly put more of our resources into its detection, and we would not write into the laws a long series of acceptable excuses, from insanity to self-defense (usefully ambiguous terms, serving in practice to allow juries, lawyers, and judges to play the game). Our equivocation in these matters no doubt reflects quite faithfully the ambivalence we feel about murder and our occasional temptations to indulge in it ourselves. Such widespread personal ambivalence or shared role-taking very likely underlies all substitution of game playing for unequivocal legal enforcement. The popular response to television programs that treat crime and law enforcement as a game of wits is another clue to our deep-seated feelings about the matter.

What distinguishes a game from other forms of competition? The essential agreement on rules which fix or shape obstacles, stakes, and penalties; agreement to accept the result for each round of play; and inability to play at all unless your opponent plays, too, either because there is then

[2] Victor A. Thompson, *The Regulatory Process in OPA Rationing* (New York, 1950).

nothing to win or because the victory is empty and unrewarding if it is won without opposition. The keynote in these rules of a game is mutual dependence, and in every one of these respects legal regulation meets the test of a game and not the test of an all-out, no-holds-barred strike for booty.

What happens psychologically when law is enforced as if it were a command rather than a virtuous generalization around which a game can be played? Instead of a trial of wits, it becomes a trial of force. Where law is treated as dogma, defiance becomes heresy; and this formulation states exactly the change in social roles and in symbolic interplay that takes place. Where enforcement is played as a game, none of those involved pretends that the offense is virtuous; but all recognize, through mutual role-taking, that there are temptations, that there is a shared interest in resisting them; and that, within the rules, offenders caught under specified conditions shall pay the specified penalties.

This pattern of symbolic interplay does not occur in our society when certain kinds of political crimes are involved. Now the offenders do claim that their crimes are virtuous, and the administrators do treat the offense, not as one to be penalized under the rules, but as one to be stamped out at all costs. Here is a heresy. Public disclaimers in its indulgence must be demanded, partly as a ritualistic assurance that every offender is being eliminated, partly to produce confusion and ambivalence among the heretics by requiring them to repeat an abstract formula they cannot sincerely embrace.

The loyalty oath or other form of proclamation of virtue neatly points up the symbolic difference between the two modes of law enforcement. It would never occur to the most zealous police official to recommend that people be required to take an oath that they will not commit murder, robbery, or battery. We all take it for granted that no one regards it as honorable to commit such crimes, but that a certain number of people will do so under sufficient provocation or temptation; a loyalty oath, even if it expresses an honest intention, can have no relevance to this kind of stress. It may, however, have a great deal of relevance to the commission of political crimes, for we take it for granted that some people do regard these acts as virtuous and honorable. Milton Rokeach makes the same point when he declares that, "dogma serves the purpose of ensuring the continued existence of the institution and the belief-disbelief system for which it stands."[3] In ordinary law enforcement, beliefs and disbeliefs are not involved: only the possibility of opportunistic advantage from beating the rules.

John Dewey similarly remarks that where law is enforced as if it were a command, it does become a trial of force.[4] It then produces overt mass resistance rather than covert individual efforts to gain an advantage by taking risks.

We may sum up this part of the argument by noting that so far as the great bulk of law enforcement is concerned "rules" are established through mutual role-taking: by looking at the consequences of possible acts from the point of view of the tempted individual and from the point of view of the impact of his acts upon the untempted. The result is a set of unchallenged rules implicitly permitting evasions and explicitly fixing penalties. Administrators are thereby able to avoid the sanctions of politically powerful groups by accepting their premises as valid; while at the same time they justify this behavior in the verbal formulas provided in the rules.

The other, less common, mode of law enforcement involves the establishment of rules asserting the exclusive validity of a belief-disbelief system which is challenged by a heresy. The function of these rules being to defend a dogma under attack, they provide for no evasions but rather for stamping out deviation through both verbal incantation and physical intimidation. Such an overt threat to the opposition

[3] Milton Rokeach, *The Open and Closed Mind* (East Lansing, Mich., 1960), p. 68.
[4] John Dewey, *The Public and Its Problems* (New York, 1927), Chap. 2.

produces resistance, further repression, and the social and personal pathologies that perceptions of strong threat evoke. Symbolically, the two kinds of law enforcement amount to the difference between mutual threat (the command) and mutual role-taking (the game).

Because the term "mutual role-taking" is fundamental to this analysis of administrative enforcement of rules, it deserves close attention. It derives, of course, from George Herbert Mead's emphasis upon the significance, both for social action and for the creation of the self, of "taking the role of the other." It is only by continuously trying to look at one's own actions from the perspective of the "significant other" person that anyone acts at all. In Mead's exposition:

By . . . taking the attitude of the other toward his own gestures . . . every gesture comes within a given social group or community to stand for a particular act or response, namely the act or response which it calls forth explicitly in the individual to whom it is addressed, and implicitly in the individual who makes it; and this particular act or response for which it stands is its meaning as a significant symbol.

Only in terms of gestures as significant symbols is the existence of mind or intelligence possible; for only in terms of gestures which are significant symbols can thinking — which is simply an internalized or implicit conversation of the individual with himself by means of such gestures — take place.[5]

Mead's work seems to me to provide the key for resolving a major dilemma of administrative theory. Herbert Simon pointed out in his early work that administrative decision-making may be conceived as a process of finding the means which will demonstrably achieve particular ends. He ultimately rejected this formulation, however, because every end is also a means to a higher, more abstract end, and as one moves higher on the means-end chain, the ends become too abstract and empty to be useful for administrators or for prediction. Simon's resolution of this problem involved a rejection of the means-end language in favor of analysis in

[5] Mead, *op. cit.*, p. 47.

terms of alternative behaviors and their consequences; but this formulation does not really eliminate the problem of a hierarchy of values, as Storing was able to show,[6] for we must still explain preferences for some consequences over others. Storing's predilection is apparently to reject completely the possibility of systematic analysis because he thinks values can neither be eliminated from any formulation nor separated from facts.

Mead's formulation suggests, however, that Simon was moving in the right direction in his behavior-consequences language. He was not wholly successful only because he did not break radically enough with normative and common-sense language. Value premises are a part of Simon's scheme, and once he introduces them, he cannot either validate them or get rid of them. Factual premises alone are certainly not sufficient to explain administrative decisional choices; but factual premises in conjunction with observable role-taking are: for the role both specifies the value premises operative in a particular instance of decision-making and establishes a probability that these same value premises will be operative in future decision-making in the same policy area. Role theory therefore offers an explanation, and a basis for prediction, of value choices without the need to establish either value hierarchies or means-end chains.

Role-taking is action. It is behavioral and observable. And, as Mead brilliantly demonstrates, it is through role-taking that significant symbols are created. If the normative political philosopher asks whether the choice of one role rather than another does not depend upon a value hierarchy, we can answer, with Mead's work and the many empirical studies based upon it as our evidence, that it is role-taking that creates the symbols in terms of which we rank values. Or, to put it another way, the ranking of values is the ra-

[6] Herbert J. Storing, "The Science of Administration: Herbert A. Simon," in H. J. Storing (ed.), *Essays on the Scientific Study of Politics* (New York, 1962), pp. 73–81.

tionalization of our behavior: an aftermath of it and not a cause. In the introduction to the second edition of *Administrative Behavior*, Simon rather gently rejects the "role" as the most useful unit of analysis, but his remarks suggest that he conceives of roles in simple dramaturgical terms. The richer Mead formulation offers a way out.

Politics always involve group conflicts. For the individual decision-maker group conflict means ambivalence, and ambivalence can be described in behavioral terms as the concomitant taking of incompatible roles. Here is the key to the "game" theory of law enforcement just discussed. Enforcers and "enforced" alike assume both the role of the potential violator and the role of his victim. Out of their responses to such mutual role-taking come the rules as actually acted out:[7] the specification of the loopholes, penalties, and rewards that reflect an acceptable adjustment of these incompatible roles. We know how "acceptability" is determined from many empirical studies of policy-making. It is a function of the sanctions available to the groups involved. Where one of the groups is organized, the rules, as enforced, are likely to be rigged so as to favor it disproportionately. Those who administer the rules in such cases become in effect part of the management of the organizations they regulate, through role-taking.

An interesting special case often occurs in local police agencies. From Lincoln Steffens' time to our own we have heard repeatedly of policemen in league with criminals, sometimes by accepting bribes in return for immunity, sometimes by actively helping in thefts. If we view administrative regulation as role-taking, it becomes quite understandable that policemen should occasionally choose this role. They are forced by their jobs to involve themselves closely both with the organization for which they work and with the one they regulate. Their every official act involves a calculation

[7] The rules as statutory or administrative language are discussed on pp. 138–145.

of its consequences for both organizations and for themselves. As this fact is clear to the criminals, too, some mutually understood rules of behavior are certain to emerge. It would be surprising indeed if these rules did not sometimes include understandings about bribery, looking the other way, and even joint enterprises. Although the ethics and the stakes may be different, the mutual role-taking is very much like what happens when staff members of regulatory commissions become part of the organizations of *their* clienteles.

It would be a mistake to believe that only individual delinquency and not organizational behavior is involved in such cases. The local police department that makes a great show of picking up lone offenders and amateur delinquents but leaves organized syndicates very much alone apart from occasional token actions is not uncommon. Even the FBI has consistently concentrated on the dramatic capture of the Dillingers, while making little headway against nationally organized gambling and other crime syndicates. The "ten most wanted criminals" device has been the dramaturgical core of FBI publicity and claims of effectiveness in its law enforcement work.[8]

Once the pattern of role-taking is established within an administrative agency it becomes self-fulfilling and self-reinforcing. This result occurs through the operation of a number of devices that students of organization have often observed; but they can be seen now as tied together through their joint function of maintaining the organization's course in line with its established role. First, there are clear value biases in hiring, in job applications, and in staff separations. This practice need not be deliberate, as it was in the TVA and NLRB of the thirties, both of which quite explicitly

---

8 The FBI illustrates in still another way that the role is a useful concept in the analysis of administrative decision-making. While its law enforcement activities constitute mutual role-taking, its attacks on political subversion exemplify mutual threat and the role of defender of dogma. This facet of FBI activity is discussed below.

used adherence to the philosophy of their respective programs as a screening device. Many staff members voluntarily left the NLRB after the enactment of Taft-Hartley because of restiveness over the new promanagement role of the agency. Civil libertarians and criminologists interested chiefly in the rehabilitation of offenders are unlikely to apply for jobs at the FBI, or to be accepted or advanced if they do apply. Richard Nixon left the wartime OPA at one stage of his career because he was uncomfortable in the liberal climate that prevailed in its offices,[9] and many liberals sought or accepted jobs at OPA for the same reason.

A second consequence of the establishment of a clear pattern of role-taking is value contagion within the agency. Each staff member who works on a case is strongly tempted to emphasize or to soft-pedal premises in line with what he knows will please or displease the people scheduled to get the docket after him. This tendency of the group to encourage conformity has been established in experimental research,[10] and it is observable in the agencies themselves as well by every employee or observer sensitive to it.

A certain number of staff members of every agency can expect to end their careers as employees or officers of the firms they are regulating, and the possibility occurs to every staff member. In some agencies, as in the FCC, government service is recognized as probably the best and most common training ground and channel for some kinds of private employment in the industry. Such an expectation is of course wholly compatible with the role-taking we are discussing, and inevitably reinforces it.[11] Not only is the individual likely to assume the role of the group into which he eventually hopes

[9] See William Costello, *The Facts About Nixon* (New York, 1960), pp. 29–30, 39.

[10] Muzafer Sherif, *The Psychology of Social Norms* (New York, 1936); Ralph M. Stogdill, *Individual Behavior and Group Achievement* (New York, 1959), pp. 78–81.

[11] See Henry W. Ehrmann, "French Bureaucracy and Organized Interests," *Administrative Science Quarterly*, Vol. 5 (March, 1961), pp. 534–555.

to graduate; in a section or bureau in which such expectations are widely held, the work group will further encourage conformity to the group's values.[12]

The status dysfunctions Barnard has catalogued and analyzed[13] contribute to the same pattern. The major consequence of these dysfunctions for decision-making is that they lead subordinates to hesitate to call attention to premises that suggest the advisability of change in established policy. As the specialists most familiar with the relevant facts are likely to be hierarchical subordinates, the result is a bias in favor of continuing to apply established policies. Anxieties of superiors stemming from their awareness of their growing incompetence as specialists may lead them to ever more rigid insistence upon uncritical adherence to the roles and policies they know.[14]

New premises disturbing to established roles may also be screened out by time-consuming routine. When every staff member finds his day taken up in checking case dockets for routine problems and premises, there is likely to be no place in the organization as a whole for innovation. March and Simon refer to this phenomenon, familiar to every bureaucrat in an old-line agency, as a Gresham's Law: ritualistic routine minimizing the likelihood of energetic search for more satisfactory solutions.[15]

Backing up all of these organizational supports of accepted roles are the agency's constituencies. We may take it as the key feature of any constituency that it can cripple or kill an agency. A congressman's constituency can fail to return him to office. Similarly, every administrative agency is at the mercy of specific groups which, given sufficient provocation, can

12 Stogdill, *op. cit.*, pp. 59–119. Peter M. Blau, *Bureaucracy in Modern Society* (Chicago, 1956), pp. 53–57.

13 Chester I. Barnard, "The Functions of Status Systems," in Robert K. Merton and others, *Reader in Bureaucracy* (Glencoe, Ill., 1952), pp. 242–254.

14 Victor A. Thompson, *Modern Organization* (New York, 1961).

15 March and Simon, *op. cit.*, p. 185.

hurt or scuttle them. Occasionally, a private group is formally given such power; labor and management organizations showed that they had it by using it several times against the War Labor Board and Wage Stabilization Board. More often Congress, the President, and the courts are the only formal constituents of administrative agencies, and it is a rare bureaucrat who does not bear the fact constantly in mind.[16] Once he has found a pattern of action which is not disturbing to these constituents and lets them turn their attentions elsewhere, he will vigorously resist any change in the pattern, for he knows where survival lies.[17]

It is the self-reinforcing policy bias of these recently recognized characteristics of organizations that is of interest here. There could hardly be a better example of Kenneth Burke's "scene-act" ratio: the recognition that acts will be consistent with the setting in which they occur.[18] It is not apparent to a casual, common-sense, or stylized inspection of administrative organizations that such policy rigidity, such built-in predilection for a built-in role, is the hallmark and core of the setting. On the contrary, the common view of administrative decision-making has emphasized a search for the most effective and efficient means to goals. This view has been common to journalistic accounts, to the proverbial approach of an earlier era of public administration study, to the early work of Simon, and to such optimistic critics as Storing and Redford. Simon heralded the end of this idealized approach in his emphasis upon limits of rationality, his comments upon "isolated subsets," and his concept of satisficing.

Both the common-sense view and the scene-act ratio have their political functions: the first to serve as a reassuring symbol evocative of an acquiescent mass public response; the second to channel resource allocations by assuring that the agency takes the role of "regulated."

[16] Murray Edelman, "Governmental Organization and Public Policy," *Public Administration Review*, Vol. 12 (Autumn, 1952), pp. 276–283.

[17] Truman, *op. cit.*, pp. 467–478.

[18] Burke, *op. cit.*, pp. 6–7.

II

Administrative agencies are to be understood as economic and political instruments of the parties they regulate and benefit, not of a reified "society," "general will," or "public interest." At the same time they perform this instrumental function, they perform an equally important expressive function for the polity as a whole: to create and sustain an impression that induces acquiescence of the public in the face of private tactics that might otherwise be expected to produce resentment, protest, and resistance. The instrumental function of administrative agencies, as defined here, has been observed, demonstrated, and documented by every careful observer of regulatory agencies.[19] This literature has nonetheless never successfully been used to challenge the widely held view and remains an esoteric facet of the study of economics and political science. The expressive function has received less attention from scholars, though the quiescence of masses in the face of demonstrable denial of what is promised them clearly calls for explanation. The last chapter has dealt with the expressive function in some detail.

Few if any norms are more deeply embedded in our culture, as verbal abstractions, than the two repeatedly cited as guiding administrative refereeing of conflict: that the weak should be protected from the strong and that conflict should be settled peacefully. Yet administrative surveillance over rival groupings commonly facilitates one of two quite different results: (a) aggrandizement by an organized group in the wake of symbolic reassurance of the unorganized, as described in the last chapter; or (b) an alliance of the ostensibly rival groupings at the expense of "outside" groups. In neither case does the regulatory agency restrict claims backed by sanctions or referee a conflict. In both cases it becomes a psychologically and organizationally effective *part* of a political constellation which possesses potent private weapons already. Specifically, it becomes that instrument of the con-

19 See p. 24.

stellation whose function it is to allay outside political protest: to provide a setting of stability and predictability within which the organized groups involved can use their weapons with minimal anxiety about counterattack. It can perform this function better than any "private" group can do it because, as a public agency, it inevitably manipulates and evokes the myths, rituals, and other symbols attaching to "the state" in our culture.

Implicit in this formulation is the view that the creation of an administrative agency in a policy area signals the emergence of a changed relationship between the groups labeled as adversaries. The agency, the regulated groups, and the ostensible beneficiaries become necessary instruments for each other while continuing to play the role of rivals and combatants. Careful examination of the nature of the change in their strategic positions clarifies the sense in which this proposition holds true. The establishment of a National Labor Relations Board, Interstate Commerce Commission, Federal Communications Commission, Office of Price Administration, or utilities commission constitutes assurance that none of the groups directly involved can push any temporary or permanent bargaining advantage to the point of eliminating the other. Certain messages are implicitly but clearly conveyed by the very creation and continued functioning of the agency, and the messages are solace for very anxious people. Unions will continue to exist as part of the American economic scene. Radio stations, railroads, airlines, and utilities will not be nationalized. Negroes will be protected in their use of economic and other weapons. Consumers are assured that the majesty of the state will protect them from the threat posed by powerful economic concentrations and sellers. In short, existing institutions are legitimized, permitting them to utilize their bargaining weapons to the full, if they have any, and to survive and comfort themselves if they have not.

To see vividly this function of an administrative agency it is helpful to consider the alternative: the situation prevailing before an agency is established in a policy area, or the situation that would prevail if an existing agency were magically abolished. We have had enough case studies of the political origins of regulatory agencies to be well aware of what is involved. A group with oligopolistic or other economic weapons at its disposal maximizes its gain, testing to learn how much the traffic will bear. This strategy creates adverse interests and anxieties: tensions and a need for their resolution on the part of both the predatory group and of its victims. Both need a definition of the situation: a legitimizing act which will remove uncertainty and the more serious anxieties in precisely the fashion I have just posited that administrative agencies do.

If the Interstate Commerce Commission, for example, were suddenly abolished, its function of maintaining and raising rates and legitimizing mergers and abandonments of service would have to be performed by the private carriers themselves. Potential customers would fear sudden and substantial changes; and the carriers themselves would fear strong public protest. Anxieties on both sides and anticipatory protest would create a degree of instability and tension that would have to be eliminated, very likely by the creation of an agency much like the ICC.

The assurance that all involved groups are legitimate and can participate at will in a joint ritual (more of administrative action as ritual shortly) constitutes a demonstration of symbiosis rather than bitter-end rivalry or parasitism. If one of the groups involved is unorganized, this is as far as the symbiosis goes. For the unorganized group the benefits are partly psychic and partly a guarantee of survival. They have the consequences for mass behavior discussed in the last chapter.

For the unorganized the administrative activity brings a change from the role of potential victims to the role of the protected: ostensible sharers with the regulated industry in the economic benefits together with a powerful showering of symbols suggesting that the new role is secure.

For those not immediately involved the same meaning is conveyed. Once it is assumed that an agency assures service and fair rates for consumers, protection of the industry against loss or destruction becomes a tactic in the protection of the industry's clients as well. A rate increase that would be rather obvious exploitation of these clients in a setting of economic infighting unrestrained by government is magically converted into help for the customers as well as the industry. Where the agency's functioning constitutes legitimizing of a claim on the national product, the same functioning symbolically involves both adversary parties as supporters of the claim. The commuter or airline passenger needs his transportation, and, by definition, the industry cannot now exploit him.

A rather more interesting symbiosis takes place where both adversary parties are organized, as in labor-management relations. Here the blood and thunder of battle, the charges and countercharges that the other group is behaving unfairly, the more or less incessant invocations of stereotyped images of the others' great strength and predatory habits, the occasional well-publicized resort to boycotts, sit-ins, and other economic and social weapons all serve to underline in the public mind the reality of the rivalry and the incompatibility of the rival interest.

It is true that there was a real effort by each adversary to crush the other for the first several decades after the industrial revolution came to the United States. Labor created such syndicalist or socialist organizations as the IWW and the Knights of Labor. Management used terrorism, espionage, its incomparably greater economic strength, and its psychological controls over judges and other public officials to break unions. This history of all-out warfare remains symbolically a part of the relationship between labor and management; but rivalry between management and labor in the go-for-broke sense disappeared at about the time administrative agencies were established in the field and was replaced by a common interest in a larger share of the national product to split between them. The new institutions did not neatly or completely replace the old ones everywhere, and the continued skirmishing effectively blinded practically everybody to the significance of the change for a long time. No group was more thoroughly blinded than those labor economists of the postwar years who had been drawn to the field in the first place by the picturesque and ideologically clean-cut in-fighting of the thirties and therefore had a large emotional stake in the thesis that the battle was real.

A major function of much union-management bargaining in the late fifties and sixties has been to provide a ritual which must be acted out as a prerequisite for the quiescent acceptance of higher prices and higher wages by those not directly involved. Nor is it surprising that the rite is most formalized precisely in the industries in which the bargaining and the speculation about the likelihood of a strike are most widely publicized: steel, autos, meat packing, heavy machinery, electronics. In these cases union-management bargaining has come close to joining such foreign institutions as codetermination and national economic councils or such domestic ones as the agreed bill process[20] as virtual giveaways both of the game and of the gross national income. The symbiosis could hardly be clearer.

In this case, as in many others, the claims made on each other by the groups involved are such that they can be satisfied by larger claims on outside groups. This drama has now been repeated so often in the industries named that its social function is manifest.

The activity of the various administrative agencies calls attention to the *distinctions* among interested groups: to concern with such different policy areas as cotton farming, air or rail transportation, or industrial relations. At the same time, as already noted, it symbolizes the common interests of groups involved as ostensible rivals in the same policy area.

[20] See Gilbert Y. Steiner, *Legislation by Collective Bargaining* (Urbana, Ill., 1951).

Through its diversified structure the administrative system thus mirrors the heterogeneity of economic and social interests in our society. In the early years of American history, when the politically significant differences among us were geographical and local ones, local and national governmental institutions mirroring this geographical diversity in interests were central. Administrative agencies were superimposed upon these and stole much of the limelight from them after the industrial revolution created the economic heterogeneities I have been discussing. The continued activity of the agencies is a symbol and a legitimizing of these various economic and social objectives. As we have seen, it marks and promotes sufficient acceptance of them that all-out attack and destruction by either ostensible opponents or outside groups is no longer expected or tolerated.

Administrative activity is effective in inducing a measure of wide acceptance of all the objectives symbolized by the agencies only because the mass public that does the accepting is ambivalent about these objectives. Its responses to events and speeches manifests both a recognition of the value of each function and anxiety about the self-seeking and predatory intentions of the economic groups profiting from them. The personification of the elements in such psychic tension, and resolution of the tension through an acting out of the contending hopes and fears, has always been a common practice in both primitive and advanced societies. To let the adversary groups oppose each other through the workings of an administrative agency continuously resolving the conflicts in "decisions" and policies replaces tension and uncertainty with a measure of clarity, meaning, confidence, and security. This is precisely the function performed in more primitive societies by the rain dance, the victory dance, and the peace pipe ceremony, each of which amounts to an acting out of contending forces that occasion widespread anxiety and a resolution that is acceptable and accepted.

Because administrative action has consequences in the form of people's responses, counterstrategies, supporting and opposing speech and activity, it is very likely to break up established political alignments and provide an impetus for new ones. An Air Force decision to abandon one missile system and adopt a different one realigns manufacturers, scientists, unions, employees, politicians, and the other armed services. As Hannah Arendt puts it, action (by which she means action with political consequences) "Has an inherent tendency to force open all limitations and cut across all boundaries."[21] It produces a chain reaction, whose ending is uncertain. That is to say, it involves and engages many groupings in one or another kind of response while at the same time demonstrating to the social scientist, through the uncertainty of the outcome and of the responses, how limited is the possibility of planning and rationality. Its political meaning is, then, both that it allocates specific tangible resources to a clearly defined group and also that it involves, through threat or reassurance, an indefinitely large mass public.

For a part of that public the abstract symbols presented by the various administrative agencies may become a stereotyped substitute for rigorous thought about their own and others' social needs. In his authoritarian personality study Adorno found that the mentally rigid types scoring high on his F and ethnocentricity scales lived in a "world of empty, schematic administrative fields."[22]

The underlying ambivalence is reflected as well in the irresolute manner in which regulations are enforced, and particularly in the predictable provision of loopholes, inefficient inspection, and devices for evasion. The realists in social science are inclined to explain such behavior as the resultant of group interest interplay; but the interplay is both psychological and social, for ambivalence, group conflict, and irresolution in law enforcement, all describe exactly the same set of responses.

[21] Hannah Arendt, *The Human Condition* (New York, 1959), pp. 169–170.
[22] Adorno and others, *op. cit.*

The administrative system is in fact a rather sensitive instrument for highlighting those political functions that are widely, if ambivalently, supported. It has time and again been necessary to change the hierarchical locus of a function precisely to facilitate such highlighting, even though there was no reason to suppose that the locational change meant a shift in policy direction or in the relative influence of interested groups. The intense lobbying in the nineteenth century by farm, business, and labor groups for their "own" cabinet departments is one expression of this phenomenon, even though in each instance the new departments at first did little or nothing not done by a bureau before, and there was even a bit of scrambling to find things for them to do. The current pressure for a Department of Urban Affairs to take over what is already being done in various other departments is another example.

Establishment of a function at the highest hierarchical level is symbolically important only where there is genuine doubt about its high valuation or political support, as in the instances just cited. Where the support is assured, as in the cases of the FBI or the Army Corps of Engineers, a shift to the highest vertical location is unnecessary and might even be impolitic in that activities of the agencies inconsistent with their symbolic claims might become conspicuous.

The creation in 1947 of a single Department of Defense is a revealing example of a shift in the name and conspicuousness of an established function without any significant corresponding change in policy or group influence. The name "defense," the single department, and the publicity accorded the activities of the Secretary of Defense and his staff highlight a function that is universally supported, as distinct from the image of rival service imperialism that had been prevalent. Larger claims on the national product are thus more easily legitimized, while the game of service imperialism need not be disturbed.

The forms benefits take also focus attention on a widely approved function rather than on the distribution of benefits to organized economic groupings. The administrative proceeding is so structured that benefits are perceived in relation to a symbolically potent and widely shared abstract objective and not in relation to their very material recipients. What we have here is a fascinating application of a well-known psychological phenomenon: that we screen percepts and interpret them in relation to a preconceived organization of reality. In administrative activity the organizing conception is very plainly presented and reiterated. It is given first in the very name of the agency. More important, it is reiterated and continuously emphasized as both proponents and opponents of specific policies justify their positions in the name of the same objective or organizing principle: a smoothly functioning transportation system or power system or communications system, rendering maximum service; the most effective defense posture; equality of management-labor bargaining power; fair trade practices; and so on.

Finally, the structure of the administrative system eliminates practically every opportunity to consider these various symbolic objectives at the same time, as rival claimants on the national product. As policy questions arise within each agency, decisions are justified in relation to the objective or organizing concept of that agency. An attack on the value of that organizing concept could come only from outside: from a different interest cluster. But this never happens in a setting in which any significant public attention to the attack could occur. It can happen only in congressional appropriation committee considerations, and there only to a slight degree and in a setting guaranteeing minimal weighing of the comparative values of alternatives even by the committee members, let alone the uninvolved public. The organizing principle retains its pristine potency.

The most valuable tangible benefits distributed by the federal government of the United States are certainly defense contracts. The form in which these become conspicuous to the uninvolved public is in defense appropriations, which highlight the universally approved defense function. That the appropriations mean high profits for the contractors is rendered inconspicuous by the political structures and modes of communication utilized. Administrative form both serves to confer an important benefit and legitimizes it through its presentation as a means of meeting a universal popular demand. There is no necessary implication here that the appropriations are not really needed for defense; only that the mode of structuring the benefit legitimize it and makes its continuation probable whether or not it serves its ostensible instrumental function.

This form of benefit is probably feasible only if the instrumental objective to be served is potent and widely shared: defense, postal service, airmail service, road construction, and so on. Where the objective is less widely shared, the form of benefit characteristically changes. A classic example is agricultural subsidies, which are so structured as to highlight a virtuous abstraction: parity. The formula by which parity payments are computed is a periodically manipulated resultant of group bargaining, and the payoffs have disproportionately gone to large and commercial farming establishments; but the administrative organization symbolizes the creation of parity.

Though parity is practically a household word to newspaper readers, its dynamics are a mystery. Congress has required at one or another time that interest, taxes, freight rates, and wages be added to the formula for computing the index of prices paid by farmers. Before 1950 there were 170 items in the index; since 1950 there have been 337. It includes forty-eight agricultural commodities, each given its own weight.[23] This weighting, inclusion, and exclusion is of course the real determinant of the benefit, not the abstraction "parity."

Another example of subsidies hidden under the guise of a popular objective are the large federal payments to publishers and advertisers in the form of second-class mail rates far lower than is necessary to cover the costs of delivering maga-

[23] Wilcox, *op. cit.*, pp. 451–452.

zines and hard-sell blurbs. Again, the subsidy may or may not be justified, depending on the observer's values, but administrative structuring has a continuing influence on the process.

Where the benefits are not to come from the public treasury at all, but rather from a grant of official permission to charge higher rates for goods or services, the administrative form is still different; but it again amounts to a ritual emphasis upon a symbolically potent objective. Benefits are still offered so that they are perceived in relation to the abstract objective and not in relation to their material recipients. Thus administrative decision-makers on the regulatory commissions function in a setting in which they become in effect part of the management of the industry they are to regulate. They are forcefully and regularly bombarded with statements of the various costs confronting the industry and with its business problems; they associate formally and often informally with its top officers, learning their perspectives and their values. At the same time they are kept intensely aware of the sanctions that await them and the agency if these business and organizational considerations are ignored: congressional displeasure, public attacks, probable displacement at the end of their terms of office. Even more obviously, their careers and prestige are now tied to the industry. As the industry grows, so does their function and importance; if the industry dies, so does the agency. Symbiosis ripens into osmosis and digestion. There is no significant difference between this situation and that of the corporation officers themselves.

The organizational and psychological embrace of the industry around the regulatory commissioners go hand in hand. To be part of the organization in the sense of incessant exposure to its problems and decisional premises is to come to share its perspectives and values. This is not "pressure"; it is absorption. It explains the inevitability of a bias in choosing value premises: a bias which has been consistently observed by students of administrative regulation. The grant of benefits in these instances has the form of elaborate due process, involving complicated and drawn out inspection of data, both in the agency's offices and in formal hearings. But the screening apparatus through which decisional premises must pass is supplied by the organizational setting and can be counted on to grind out its foreordained result regardless of the awesomeness of the procedures. The latter serve quite another function: not so much to build rational calculations of the consequences of alternative decisions, as to legitimize what finally is announced by emphasizing the care with which it is related to the agency's symbolic objective. Occasional decisions slapping the industry but not altering the major trend further bolster the symbolism, for the commissioners themselves as much as for the mass public.

One type of procedural requirement is especially revealing. The legislature has flatly proscribed the gathering of particular kinds of data by some agencies. A rather flagrant example of this occurs in the Taft-Hartley Act, which forbids the National Labor Relations Board to employ staff members for economic analysis, forbids the hearing examiner from making recommendations in representation cases,[24] and forbids the trial examiner in unfair labor practice cases from being present when the board considers the case at which he presided. Such provisions quite explicitly bar the board from paying overt attention to certain types of data or points of view, particularly facts and values growing out of observation of what occurred, or allegedly occurred, in the plant. The board is thus encouraged to behave less like an investigating administrative agency and more like a court, confining its attention chiefly to past interpretations of the law. Such ignoring of actual behavior in the plant is practically certain to mean overlooking much of the evidence that an employer charged with an unfair labor practice did things which indicate he has an anti-union bias. It is therefore not hard to understand why employer groups favored these procedural innovations in the Taft-Hartley law and unions opposed them.

[24] Act of June 23, 1947, Public Law 101, 80th Congress, 1st Session, 29 U.S. Code, Chap. 7, Subchap. II, Secs. 151–168, Sec. 4(a).

Another example of this device appeared in a rider attached to the law appropriating Federal Trade Commission funds for 1954. In this instance Congress stipulated that "no part of the foregoing appropriation shall be available for a statistical analysis of the consumer's dollar." [25]

While the pro-employer bias of the Taft-Hartley provisions is clear, they could not very often prevent the board from learning about significant anti-union behavior in the plant or other relevant information. Their effect, rather, is exactly what they purport to provide: to limit the publicizing of certain kinds of information *as part of the formal record and proceedings*. They thereby keep the rite unsullied when the NLRB or the FTC makes decisions of the kind pro-business congressmen hope for. To keep it unsullied is to preserve its sanctifying power in fuller potency.

The administrative system, as symbol and ritual, thus serves as legitimizer of elite objectives, as reassurance against threats, and sometimes as catalyst of symbiotic ties between adversaries. It should not be surprising that we find these larger social functions of the administrative system mirrored inside each of the agencies as well, in the gathering and choice of premises upon which decisions are based.

Simon and others have demonstrated that complete rationality in decision-making is never possible in any case: because knowledge of the consequences of any course of action is always fragmentary, because future values cannot be anticipated perfectly, and because only a very few of the possible alternative courses of action ever come to mind.[26] By observing how administrative staff members are themselves guided in their work by the compelling symbols the system serves, we can go a considerable way toward defining the particular biases or policy directions which these limits upon rationality take. We can, that is, hope to observe some systematic patterns in departures from administrative rationality. The earlier section of this chapter has tried to do that.

[25] Public Law 176, July 31, 1953.
[26] Herbert A. Simon, *Administrative Behavior* (New York, 1958), p. 81.

III

If role theory is useful in explaining administrative policy in allocating tangible resources, it is equally so in explaining administrative intervention into political conflicts that center around intangible threats: the second of the modes of regulation and law enforcement identified earlier in this chapter. The most striking behavior of the agency engaged in fighting an intangible threat lies, in fact, in its avid courting of publicity and in the flamboyance with which it asserts its choice of role. This contrasts with the inconspicuous style in which the agency involved in tangible resource allocations finds a viable course of action.

We have already noticed that mutual threat is the symbolic keynote of administrative regulation where a dogma and a heresy confront each other. Each ideological assertion aggravates the heretical and dogmatic character of the other, as in the series of political conflicts in American history centering around alleged threats from alien churches, nations, and social programs. It is worth underlining the fact that the political benefits directly flowing from such a struggle are intangible, involving the status and legitimacy of those who hold political ideologies. If the stakes were not so evanescent, the enforcement behavior would very likely be less dramatic. The stakes are intangible, of course, not in the sense that the benefits involved are insignificant but rather in the sense that the reality of the threat is itself unverifiable and the subject of dispute.

It is hardly surprising that administrative activity in such a setting should consist largely of assertions of the reality and mammoth proportions of the threat. Let us take, as a polar example of this sort of administrative action, the record of the FBI in respect to communism in the four decades that followed the first World War. This record has consisted through the whole of this period of repeated and highly publicized declarations of two theses: (1) that the communist "conspiracy" in the United States has never been stronger or more dangerous; and (2) that the FBI has never been more vigorous and effective in coping with it.[27]

These messages have been disseminated through both words and action. On the one hand there has been a great deal of speech-making, both by J. Edgar Hoover and by others, and there has been a series of reports from the FBI, committees of Congress concerned with internal security, the American Legion, and other private organizations in the threat-maximizing-and-defending role. These addresses and papers have cited statistics on the impressive number of sup-porters and dupes of the conspiracy and have told heroic tales of FBI vigilance and success.

At the same time highly publicized actions conveying the same messages to the convinced and to some of the unaligned have periodically taken place: "slacker" raids, Palmer raids, arrests of leading communists and raids on their headquar-ters, the Sacco-Vanzetti case, the Hiss trial, the Smith Act trials, and so on. It is common to all these actions that they have become evocative symbols of history just as they were rituals of ideological conflict when they took place. What they "showed" is as much a topic of controversy now as it was then. Their political consequence was to harden both the dogma and the heresy, to "prove," depending on one's role, either the reality of the threat arising from the Communist conspiracy, or the reality of the threat arising from persecu-tion of liberals under the subterfuge of an alien conspiracy. These responses from both groups of role-takers are clear, strong, and easily observable.

Far from reflecting mutual role-taking, then, the FBI mili-tantly aligns itself with one of the adversary groups. From the behavior we observe we can only conclude that it is psycho-logically and politically necessary for the agency in this posi-tion to emphasize both the threat and the protection against the threat its activity affords. In the degree that this view of

27 Donald F. Whitehead, *The FBI Story; A Report to the People* (New York, 1956); Max Lowenthal, *The Federal Bureau of Investigation* (New York, 1950).

the agency's function is accepted, the survival and expansion of the agency is assured. Role-taking therefore serves the same function for this kind of agency as it does for the agency that allocates tangible resources.

Unambiguous alignment with one of the adversary groups, as in the FBI case, cannot possibly bring the support of all or even nearly all of the population. The function of such alignment is to polarize and not to persuade. If there were no differences among the public on the reality of the communist threat or the appropriate methods of coping with it, it would of course no longer be an issue and would be of no use to the FBI. It is precisely the polarization that pits dogma against heresy and enables the FBI to play its role. The greater the polarization the more convincing the role. In this light the emphasis we notice upon the alleged threat and upon the potency of the alleged protections the FBI offers are hardly surprising.

It is also apparent that only an intangible threat permits this kind of administrative role-taking. In the measure that a threat is clearly observable and subject to systematic study, perceptions of its character and of techniques for dealing with it converge. Polarization and exaggeration become less feasible.

As either mutual role-taking or the role of defender of a dogma are basic to the survival of administrative organizations, any analysis of their choice of decisional premises which does not begin with analysis of these roles is bound to be imprecise and unpredictive. The role provides the key patterning in the selection and rejection of premises.

The administrative system, seen in this perspective, involves considerably more than the ministerial mechanics or statics of the common view. It mirrors, reinforces, and sometimes helps realign the major interest groupings of society and by the same token mirrors deep ambivalences in all of us.

All the activities of an agency taken together, and not any one pronouncement or act, perform these functions. Conflicts among group interests and within individuals find a reflection in an on-going series of verbal declarations, actions, resource allocations, and other symbols. Each of these supplement, reinforce, legitimize, qualify, and rationalize the others in a never-ending search to reflect current group alignments. So it is the sum total of the behaviors of a public agency — procedures, decisions, dicta, past policies and reputation, anticipations of future policies, dissents — that constitute the response to interest interplay, and not any one of these.

Dissent is especially revealing in this respect. The view just stated implies that dissenters on administrative commissions and courts serve a necessary function in the sense that if they do not exist, they are created, and perhaps even in the further sense that if their dissents were the majority policy, they would not necessarily take the same position. The dynamics of this process are impossible to see, and it must therefore remain a speculation; but we have probably been under-valuing some evidence that suggests it. It cannot be sheer chance that there is almost always one, and almost always only one, FCC commissioner who chronically dissents from the decisions of his colleagues that vest highly lucrative rights in the public domain in established licensees. There always is an Irwin Stewart, Lawrence Fly, Clifford Durr, or Freida Hennock; but the function of these people is to voice a politically feeble protest against the dominant pattern, not to make policy, and above all not to gain much support.

There is no reason to suppose that any single pattern of administrative acts-plus-symbols is the only one that will adequately reflect group interest interplay at a particular time. It can be taken for granted, however, that a change in any of the facets of administrative action necessitates some change in the other facets in order to retain a configuration or transaction that is socially and psychologically adequate.

CHAPTER 4

Political Leadership

Recent research on leadership suggests that "leadership" may be the wrong word. The word connotes an individual free to choose his course of action and able to induce others to follow his lead because of his superior intelligence, knowledge, skill, and the force of his personality. The emphasis in modern leadership theory is rather upon the willingness of followers to follow. The implication is that the leader's choices are quite narrowly prescribed by followers' demands and that no set of individual traits adds up to a general ability to lead, though specific traits may be helpful in particular situations.[1] Leadership is a complex and subtle thing, and we are learning to look for its dynamics in mass responses, not in static characteristics of individuals.

The reaction of large publics to leaders is rarely a simple, rational judgment that the leader can get his followers what they want and therefore should be followed. Governmental leaders have tremendous potential capacity for evoking strong emotional response in large populations. When an individual is recognized as a legitimate leading official of the state, he becomes a symbol of some or all the aspects of the state: its capacity for benefitting and hurting, for threatening and reassuring. His acts, for this reason, are public in character. They are perceived as having significant, strong, enduring,

[1] For a good review and bibliography of leadership theory see Warren G. Bennis, "Leadership Theory and Administrative Behavior," *Administrative Science Quarterly*, Vol. 4 (December, 1959), pp. 259–301.

indirect consequences for large numbers of people. As John Dewey has pointed out in one of his most useful insights, such perception of actions as having important and continuing indirect consequences for a group is precisely what marks the pragmatic distinction between private acts and public ones.[2]

In this light the belief of classical and renaissance dramatists that only rulers can be depicted as the leading figures in tragedy reveals some measure of political sophistication. The ruler's acts are public in the sense that they involve the fate of large populations, and his downfall can be tragic when interests of general public concern are thereby defeated. A changed polity and some new conceptions of dramatic possibility have enabled modern playwrights to make tragic figures of the salesman and the housewife, but only because the dilemmas these characters fail to resolve also involve and defeat large populations.

In an age of large organizations the decisions of officials about the allocation of tangible resources to groups of the population are controlled far more than in simpler polities by the factual and value premises assembled through organization. Individuals may differ in the quickness with which they recognize what is required, but maneuverability is severely limited, even for the highest officials, by the information the organization supplies and screens. In short, the difference between two political leaders in the same position today rests relatively little on differences in policy direction and very largely on other behaviors which we can label "leadership styles." Leaders rely increasingly on style differences to create and emphasize an impression of maneuverability, and the impression remains an important political fact even if the maneuverability is not.

The achievement of particular results is therefore not ordinarily a major influence upon the continued incumbency of a leader or upon public restiveness or satisfaction, though it may become so in rare cases of inflexibility or obtuseness.

[2] Dewey, *op. cit.*, pp. 12–13.

What counts normally is the affective response of political groupings in particular situations.

Leadership, then, is not to be understood as something an individual does or does not have, at all times and places. It is always defined by a specific situation and is recognized in the response of followers to individual acts and speeches. If they respond favorably and follow, there is leadership; if they do not, there is not.

This highly specific, operational character of leadership becomes badly obscured in the modern state. A major cause of confusion is the common practice of describing leadership and referring to it in terms of the traits of an elite. Such description masquerades as social science or objective analysis of leadership; but it is patently an ideology, creating the impression that some people are born to be leaders in all situations and others to follow where the wise and the courageous lead them. Such pseudoscientific discussion also moves easily to the assumption that those in high political and organizational positions in fact possess the elite traits leaders are supposed to have. These impressions are ideal for inducing docility and quiescence, for they suggest that those in charge know best and act most successfully. This is a *status quo* ideology, a special case of the view that whatever is is right.[3]

The confounding of leadership and incumbency is at the heart of mass response to political acts in a more basic sense. Incumbency in a top hierarchical position is commonly referred to as a position of leadership, without any inquiry into whether there is a following for specific acts. It is usually difficult or impossible to trace the tangled objective consequences of political acts and to know whether an individual's course has hurt or helped a group an official represents. The confusion between leadership and incumbency, together with the uncertain effects of an incumbent's course of action, frequently produces uncritical popular acclaim for an incumbent, not tied in any way to his verifiable effectiveness in furthering his constituents' interests.

[3] Thompson, *Modern Organization*, pp. 118–122.

An incumbent and his constituents today are organizationally and psychologically separated from each other to a degree
that is far more divisive than the geographical separation
characteristic of the early nineteenth century. Thomas Jefferson's constituents found it much harder to get to Washington
than we do and did not hear news summaries on the hour;
but those who cared could more easily reach an accurate
opinion on the implications for their own interests of the
Louisiana Purchase or strict construction of the Constitution
than we can reach on the implications for our interests of a
decision to test nuclear bombs in the atmosphere, raise the
national debt limit, or sell a large block of stock in a point-to-
point space communications corporation to the American
Telephone and Telegraph Company. The clue to what is
politically effective is to be found not so much in verifiable
good or bad effects flowing from political acts as in whether
the incumbent can continue indefinitely to convey an impression of knowing what is to be done.

A line of political thinking from Marx through Durkheim
and Freud to the mass society theorists explains a good deal
of why this political strategy has been so effective for presidents and congressional leaders in recent years. Alienation,
anomie, despair of being able to chart one's own course in a
complex, cold, and bewildering world have become characteristic of a large part of the population of advanced countries. As the world can be neither understood nor influenced,
attachment to reassuring abstract symbols rather than to one's
own efforts becomes chronic. And what symbol can be more
reassuring than the incumbent of a high position who knows
what to do and is willing to act, especially when others are
bewildered and alone? Because such a symbol is so intensely
sought, it will predictably be found in the person of any
incumbent whose actions *can* be interpreted as beneficent,
whether it is because they are demonstrably beneficent or
because their consequences are unknowable. Little wonder
that Eisenhower, Kennedy and Johnson have been able to
maintain remarkably high Gallup poll ratings throughout

their administrations, the ratings dropping somewhat on the rather rare occasions that the president took decisive action hurting a specific group, but recovering quickly as the consequences of the action dissipated in a maze of tertiary effects and untraceable feedback.

Max Weber has drawn the classic distinction between bureaucratic and charismatic leadership.[4] What is involved in the "leadership" just described, however, is neither bureaucratic nor charismatic. It does not rely, like the ideal-type bureaucratic leader, upon strictly rational routines to determine decisions, for the key influences are not routine and determinable results, but mass reassurances. Nor does it rely, like the charismatic leader, upon extraordinary personal qualities, demonstrable success, and dramatic smashing of routines to demonstrate the genius of the leader. It depends rather upon the impossibility of demonstrating success or failure, a disinclination to rock the boat, and the disposition of alienated masses to project their psychic needs upon incumbents of high office. Our environment of large organizations, our media for disseminating a barrage of abstract symbols, and our detachment from warm personal relationships provide a culture that is generating a new leadership dynamics.

Fundamental to this dynamics is the general sense of anxiety about the comprehensive function played in human affairs by chance, ignorance, and inability to comprehend, plan, and take responsibility for remote and complicated contingencies. The evidence that such anxiety is now common and intense is to be found in a large and growing literature of psychiatric and sociological studies and is graphically presented in Erich Fromm's *Escape from Freedom*.[5] The manner in which men have reacted in recent decades to incumbents of high political office who appear to be in command of the situation supports the conclusion that seems reasonable on a

[4] Hans H. Gerth and C. Wright Mills, *From Max Weber: Essays in Sociology* (New York, 1958), pp. 246 ff.
[5] Fromm, *op. cit.*

priori grounds: that the public official who dramatizes his competence is eagerly accepted on his own terms. The illusion is created that planning of consequences and of the future is possible in far greater degree than it demonstrably is.

Because it is apparently intolerable for men to admit the key role of accident, of ignorance, and of unplanned processes in their affairs, the leader serves a vital function by personifying and reifying the processes. As an individual, he can be praised and blamed and given "responsibility" in a way that processes cannot. Incumbents of high public office therefore become objects of acclaim for the satisfied, scapegoats for the unsatisfied, and symbols of aspirations or of whatever is opposed. To them are constantly ascribed careful weighing of alternatives and soul-searching decisions. That the premises for the decisions are largely supplied and screened by others and the decision itself frequently predetermined by a succession of subordinates' decisions is not publicized. Decision-making at the highest levels is not so much literal policy-making as dramaturgy.

George Gallup has called attention to a kind of variation in presidential popularity that is difficult to explain except by a theory of the kind just advanced. He told an interviewer:

I would say that any sharp drop in popularity is likely to come from the President's inaction in the face of an important event. Inaction hurts a President more than anything else. A President can take some action, even a wrong one, and not lose his popularity. One of the great mysteries of the political scene last year was why President Kennedy did not suffer a great loss of popularity after the Cuban setback. But he didn't. People tend to judge a man by his goals, by what he's trying to do, and not necessarily by what he accomplishes or by how well he succeeds. People used to tell us over and over again about all the things that Roosevelt did wrong and then they would say, "I'm all for him, though, because his heart is in the right place; he is trying." . . . If people are convinced you are trying to meet problems and that you are aware of their problems and are trying to do something about them, they don't hold you responsible for 100 per cent success. Nor do you have to have any great ideas on how to accomplish the ends.[6]

Willingness to cope is evidently central. Any action substitutes personal responsibility for impersonal causal chains and chance.

The assumption of responsibility becomes vital in a world that is impossible to understand or control, but the manner in which leaders are held "responsible" is highly revealing. It is expected of the top executive of every large organization that he will periodically proclaim his willingness, even eagerness, to take personal responsibility for the acts, and especially the mistakes, of his subordinates. Each time this stylized manifesto appears everyone involved experiences a warm glow of satisfaction and relief that responsibility has been assumed and can be pinpointed. It once again conveys the message that the incumbent is the leader, that he knows he is able to cope, and that he should be followed.

In practice, however, it turns out that this message is the only one such ritualistic assumption of "responsibility" conveys. It emphatically does not mean that the chief executive will be penalized for the mistakes of subordinates or that the latter will not be penalized. On the contrary, it is ordinarily only the subordinates who suffer for mistakes. It is they who are fired, denied promotion or demoted, or haled before a congressional committee to explain and be publicly castigated.[7] So clear is the general understanding that the hierarchical chief benefits rather than suffers from the assumption of "responsibility" that his political opponents are outraged when, in a specific incident, he refuses to allow a subordinate to be identified and says he will shoulder responsibility himself. All concerned then understand that no one will in fact suffer at all and that the chief executive has scored heavily.

[6] *Opinion Polls: Interviews by Donald McDonald with Elmo Roper and George Gallup* (Santa Barbara, Calif., 1962), pp. 34–35.
[7] Cf. Thompson, *Modern Organization*, pp. 129–137.

Attacks on the incumbent of a high political office do not detract from the impression of his potency as a leader. Indeed, attacks are probably more influential in promoting such an impression than support or praise for his actions. The attacker is in fact assuring all concerned that the incumbent is acting and that he is powerful. The additional message that the attacker does not like the incumbent or what he is doing makes all the more credible his assertion that the incumbent is powerfully influencing events. As Gallup points out, that assertion is precisely what most of the spectators want, whether they like the policy directions taken or not.

Because so many influences converge to dramatize an incumbent's leadership and because his success or failure is so difficult to assess, an office holder may adopt successfully either an active or a passive style if he knows how to carry it off. He may be a Roosevelt, rather frequently taking clear policy lines in behalf of, or against, specific groups, or he may be an Eisenhower, relying largely on the influences mentioned above to maintain his leadership role. The active style is very likely easier to carry off when emergency conditions are objectively present: a hot war or a major depression. Success in winning a following for programs involving substantial immediate deprivations for a sizable group is likely to be a function of threat perceptions among followers. In the degree that means of coping with the emergency are unknown, belief in the leader's magical ability to cope is doubtless enhanced because it is so intensely sought, and uncritical acquiescence becomes the response. The leader must know how to take advantage of this psychological reaction. A Roosevelt dramatizes both the seriousness of the depression and the emergency character of his remedies. A Hoover denies that a serious depression exists or that extraordinary acts are called for and thereby denies himself a following.

The passive style, however, is probably the more revealing about contemporary politics, both because it is a rather recent development as a device to achieve leadership and popularity and because it is not often discussed in the extant leadership studies. It consists basically of the avoidance of firm positions on controversial subjects while at the same time posturing as protagonist against an evanescent enemy, thereby retaining or increasing political support from large numbers of antagonists on both sides of controversies. Such a leader may declare he will support the law of the land while refusing to endorse the morality of the Supreme Court desegregation decision. He may, like Kennedy, firmly and frequently declare that the government has a responsibility to support prosperity and quicken economic growth while refraining from embarking on controversial economic policies to increase productivity or cut unemployment. The chief executive may maintain his "symbolic leadership" through ascriptions of his ability to cope, through publicized action on noncontroversial policies or on trivia, and through a dramaturgical performance emphasizing the traits popularly associated with leadership: forcefulness, responsibility, courage, decency, and so on.

Thus, Hyman and Sheatsley concluded from survey research that "Eisenhower's lack of commitments at this time simply encourage his supporters to see him either as a nonpartisan national leader, or as an unspoken sympathizer with their own views." [8] It is wholly in line with the findings of experimental and empirical research on perception to conclude that in an ambiguous situation people may, as the result of their own anxieties, perceive a leader's acts to be what they want them to be. Harry Stack Sullivan observed that such screening of what is perceived in order to avoid increased anxiety regularly occurs, and he labeled it "selective inattention." [9]

An analysis of some occasions on which leaders are displaced clarifies these observations and indicates some limits and qualifications. I suggest that the basic condition for the

[8] Herbert H. Hyman and Paul B. Sheatsley, "The Political Appeal of President Eisenhower," *Public Opinion Quarterly*, Vol. 17 (Winter, 1953–54), pp. 443–460.

[9] Harry Stack Sullivan, *The Interpersonal Theory of Psychiatry* (New York, 1953), pp. 170, 346–347.

displacement of political leadership is the leader's inability or lack of opportunity to convey the impression of coping with an opposition that can be identified and personified. An incumbent American president has more to fear from an economic recession at election time than from any other condition. There is ample evidence that the "ins" suffer from recession whether they are demonstrably responsible or not.[10] It is apparently not deprivation in itself that produces such disillusionment with leaders, for in other situations, such as a hot war, deprivation is accepted as underlining the seriousness of the obstacles with which the leader is bravely coping and, if anything, increases his following. In a war, however, the enemy is identified and visibly under attack. A leader whose acts suggest that he has a strategy and is pursuing it finds it easy to attract a loyal and enthusiastic following. The case of Neville Chamberlain in 1939 and 1940 illustrates the point, for Chamberlain's loss of a following came about precisely because his acts indicated he was not sure who the enemy was; after events had shown his lack of acumen on that score, he gave no evidence of ability to cope or of a strategy.

In a recession or depression, however, the enemy consists of economic forces much more difficult to personify or even to identify, so that a leader finds it hard to demonstrate his capacity for attacking them. There is a strong chance the incumbent will look impotent. Because depression is dangerous to leadership, the temptation is very strong for presidents to deny that its symptoms are serious; but this gambit weakens the opportunity to demonstrate ability to act, and in the face of objective hardship and widespread deprivation can be taken as conclusive proof of incapacity. Franklin Roosevelt showed his political acumen by identifying himself with the view that the depression was a major catastrophe, in opposition to the Hoover line that it was a temporary readjustment; and he personified the enemy with the argument that acts of

[10] See Louis H. Bean, *How to Predict Elections* (New York, 1948), p. 24.

the Republican administration and of big business were responsible for the disaster. This dramaturgical difference between Roosevelt and Hoover was considerably more important politically than any difference in their actual attacks upon the depression. It has often been pointed out that the Hoover administration began many of the New Deal policies. This was to be expected, for many of the same decisional premises were already present.

By denying himself an enemy and a chance to stage a battle Hoover became one of the very few presidents of recent times to fail to win reelection when he sought it. In view of the many advantages an incumbent enjoys in his effort to win a following and thereby become a leader, we should expect incumbents to defeat challengers most of the time, and they have done so. There have been ten opportunities in the twentieth century for incumbent presidents to be defeated, but it has happened only twice. On the only other occasion William Howard Taft suffered from a major split in his party. The fact that each major party has won seven of the fourteen presidential contests of the twentieth century serves as a rough control for the importance of party organization.

A comparison of this record with the recent experiences of incumbent state governors offers further evidence for the view that it helps an incumbent to be able to convey the impression of coping with an identifiable opposition in his official acts. The problems that create the greatest anxieties in the contemporary world are those with which the national government deals. This state of affairs offers presidents ample opportunity to act in the grand manner, but at the same time often denies it to the governors of the states. The latter must spend much of their time on administrative chores in which there is little popular interest. The gubernatorial acts which have often impinged most tellingly on public attention in the years since World War II have been recommendations for higher taxes to meet the steeply rising costs of relief, education, highways, and other state services. Here again are major deprivations flowing from impersonal trends, with no enemy in sight. Other, more dramatic issues, do arise in the various states, of course, and politically astute governors can make the most of them. On the whole, however, an incumbent governor cannot take it for granted that he will benefit automatically from incumbency in the way a president does, with the result that there is no clear pattern in the reelection or defeat of incumbents, as there is in the presidency. In both 1958 and 1960 almost as many governors who ran for reelection were defeated as won. These conclusions suggest that the tie is tenuous indeed between the objective interests of groups of constituents and their reasons for choosing to follow or to defeat an incumbent.

How important this conclusion is for public policy depends in part on how incumbents of high political office are chosen in our polity. Is there anything about the process that makes likely the selection of people who will be responsive to particular groups, or to all groups, even though they do not have to be responsive in order to retain their offices?

Though the process is certainly not systematic to any high degree, we have observations that point to some systematic biases. Put together, they suggest some significant conclusions. First, there is a large overlap between economic and professional leaders and people who take an active part in politics. This is true for income, occupation, education, and other measures of socioeconomic status.[11]

A second element develops from the tie between personality and culture. Charles Morris declares:

A culture, as a preference for certain modes of behavior, involves a preference for certain personality structures rather than others; the kind of person favored in one group may be condemned in another. And those whose personality is looked down upon in a given society constitute one reservoir of resistance to social control and a dynamic source of possible social change. For the sign-processes of a given individual are inevitably subject to correction in terms of the reliability and adequacy of the signs with respect to his own observations and needs, and this is as true of

11 Lane, *op. cit.*, p. 93.

socially implanted signs as of other signs; the deviant individual
is simply one in which this process of correction will be strongest
Because of this it is a false picture to assume that "society" simply
molds a passive individual to its pattern.[12]

It seems reasonable, and also accords with what evidently
happens in politics, that people with the approved personality structure are much more likely than others to be selected
by slating committees for elective office and also stand a
better chance of winning high appointive offices. They are
also more likely, once in office, to convey the impression of
capacity to cope. This phenomenon has a chiefly negative implication for policy formation. It can be counted on to minimize social experimentation and innovation if Morris is right
that those whose personality is looked down upon are the
most likely people to seek social change. It cannot be expected to produce equitable representation of policy interests,
for personality structure is involved, not a rational judgment
of interest representation.

Personality structure enters into the selection of leadership
in another way. Every person's "self" can be understood as a
taking of the roles of other people around him who become
significant for him. Which roles an individual takes may
depend upon early experiences or other things; but personality consists of such personal interactions and of nothing
more, according to such leading theorists as Mead and Sullivan.[13] It follows that the groups into which an individual
chooses to inject himself may determine, influence, or change
his personality structure, or may influence his style of action
and the values he holds. It is commonplace for an individual
newly appointed to a position in an organization to take on
rather quickly the values and modes of response of his prede-
cessor, even though he may have derided and attacked them
while still an outsider.

In an important study of symbolism Markey makes the fol-

[12] Charles Morris, *Signs, Language and Behavior* (New York, 1946),
p. 209.
[13] Mead, *op. cit.*; Sullivan, *op. cit.*

lowing comment: "In view of the facts regarding the control of the individual by the group it is evident that persons themselves, by controlling the stimuli to which they will be subjected and the groups to which they belong, can thereby create in themselves different personalities. The possibilities, of course, are conditioned by their past equipment and the possibility of controlling the stimuli to which they will be subjected." [14] Similarly, Sherif declares, paraphrasing a finding of William Foot Whyte in his study of "Street Corner Society": "The higher up a member is in the hierarchy, the greater is the strength of the demand on him to live up to the expectations of other members. Otherwise he is likely to be dropped down in the hierarchy of positions." [15]

Many people are quite consciously aware of this factor and shape their careers accordingly. Others may sense that it is an influence upon their lives, without consciously manipulating their actions to take advantage of it. It explains, however, why it is fairly common in today's highly organized society for individuals to refuse "higher" posts, especially administrative ones, knowing that acceptance would require them to become different people than they want to be. A new organizational position would be especially likely to require that they give up or discount values that are important to them in their existing organizational and social positions.

Clearly, there is a systematic bias at work here in the selection of leaders. In the degree that self-selection of roles and therefore of personality is possible, people who are quite willing to adapt themselves to the values and styles that appeal to the groups that wield sanctions select themselves for high office. Those who are less flexible in these respects are more likely to avoid it. To move upward in the political or administrative hierarchy is to be willing in some degree to be flexible by adopting ideas that are popular with the influen-

[14] John F. Markey, *The Symbolic Process and Its Integration in Children* (New York and London, 1928), p. 170.
[15] Muzafer Sherif, *An Outline of Social Psychology* (New York, 1948), p. 102.

tial and forgetting those that are not. The "influential" may, for a particular office, be the majority of the voters; in other cases it may be a small elite group.

For some offices and some individuals flexibility may not be especially important because an appointee may already have an inflexible attachment to the very preferences and styles of action that are most strongly approved in the organization in question. If the Director of the Central Intelligence Agency is an authoritarian and rigid type, unswerving in his pursuit of conservative values, this personality may be quite suitable for success in his post, though it might bring quick rejection if he ran for elective office or were appointed to head the Council of Economic Advisers or the National Bureau of Standards. In these two agencies the staff consists largely of professionals and specialists accustomed to wide freedom in doing their work and reporting their findings, and they would resist an administrator who tried to encroach on these prerogatives.

There are, of course, other explanations, having no apparent systematic value bias, of the decisions of particular individuals to seek governmental office. Intrapsychic tension, or conflicting rationalizations for differing behavior patterns in a society, often encourages withdrawal from political participation, but sometimes may lead to power-seeking as a way to quiet doubts through the actual exercise of power.[16]

From the perspective of the general public the question of whom to support as a political leader appears in a different light. The reasons particular individuals have become prominent or have felt it important to achieve high office are not the important data, as they are to the individuals themselves. The mass public is rather in the position of being asked to make a choice among a comparatively small group of aspirants, who are presented to its attention. A very large number of other people possess qualifications as good or better than those under consideration. Many of these are "unavailable"

[16] Harold D. Lasswell, *Power and Personality* (New York, 1948), p. 49; Lane, *op. cit.*, p. 116.

in the sense that their occupational, religious, racial, ethnic, sexual, or other identifications are thought by party leaders to be inappropriate. Many others, however, are simply inconspicuous. They have never taken part in public life and have never come to general public attention, though they may be prominent and highly effective in their own organizational and social circles.

Although there is obviously no systematic canvass of all the available talent in selecting people for elective or appointive posts, and although a large fraction of the talent is systematically rejected for reasons other than their qualifications, the impression is assiduously cultivated and apparently widely accepted that the candidates under active consideration represent the carefully winnowed pick of the crop. In the degree that this impression is conveyed an election arouses the necessary interest to make it an effective rite celebrating popular participation; and in the case of both appointive offices and elective ones the impression helps induce public quiescence.

The impression is not hard to convey for, as John Dewey noted, the fact that a man is conspicuous is what makes him a potential candidate for high public office.[17] Nor does it much matter for what reason he has become conspicuous so long as his achievements are generally regarded as respectable. A man who becomes conspicuous in a field other than politics is regarded as especially available if his achievement has been unusual or heroic. Victorious generals have been the most common example, but in recent years the man who first orbited the earth in an American space capsule was promptly discussed as a candidate for high political office; and the manufacturing executive who pioneered in producing and marketing the compact automobile soon became a candidate for the governorship of Michigan and was widely discussed as an aspirant for the presidency. A figure firmly established as one of the select number of leading candidates for high office

17 Dewey, *op. cit.*, pp. 78–82.

apparently benefits from some of the same attributions of leadership traits as do incumbents.

Taken together, these various influences on the emergence of incumbents of high public office and on their personalities militate toward their acceptance of the group values that are already dominant.

We can similarly formulate some tentative propositions about the demographic origins and the values of leaders of political movements that challenge established elites or take advantage of new power opportunities. Central to the kind of theory that is most useful here is the anthropological concept of marginality. The man who is identified with two social classes or other incompatible social groupings is far more likely than the clearly identified individual to become dissatisfied with approved, long established ways of thought and to recognize opportunities for winning support for policy innovations, challenges to elites, or syntheses of ideas long thought incompatible. Intellectuals, whose education and occupation often make them marginal, are especially likely to perform such a function. In the passage quoted earlier Morris explains such behavior in terms of the insistence of the deviant individual upon correcting common sign processes. Karl Mannheim offers an explanation more closely in line with the marginality concept: "A group whose class position is more or less definitely fixed already has its political viewpoint decided for it. Where this is not so, as with the intellectuals, there is a wider area of choice and a corresponding need for total orientation and synthesis. . . . Only he who really has the choice has an interest in seeing the whole of the social and political structure." [18]

While the leadership of resistance or protest movements undoubtedly also benefits from attributions of charisma and of whatever qualities are admired and sought after by its followers, such leaders depend to a greater degree than incumbents of high governmental positions upon the ability of the

[18] Karl Mannheim, *Ideology and Utopia* (New York, 1952), p. 143.

leader to recognize opportunities for policy innovation and the exercise of power. In view of this analysis it is not surprising that the most careful studies of leadership conclude that leadership and official headship are not only different, but incompatible.[19]

The appeal of the public official exists fundamentally because of what he symbolizes to his followers, and though some of the dimensions of this interaction have already been mentioned, the process can be specified a little more clearly. Duncan observes that "Through symbols we intensify or enlarge the impression of the personality, because we are able to identify with the self those symbols which have been given power by community use. . . . The resonance of symbols, the sensuous as well as intellectual attention evoked, supplies the individual with means by which he can enlarge or intensify his sphere of power."[20]

Incumbency insures wide attention, sensuous and intellectual, for those who wish to use it evocatively and have the dramatic skill; and incumbents of high governmental office naturally find it easier than others to "identify with the self those symbols which have been given power by community use." Because the mass audience paying attention to acts is larger, these propositions hold best for occupants of conspicuous national office and for those officials who can resonate remote and abstract symbols: the President, the general, the Supreme Court Justice, the chief international negotiator, the majority leaders in Congress, the Director of the FBI. We feel we know these figures in a way we usually do not know the personalities of local councilmen, the mayor, or the police chief. Our "knowledge" of the national officials in question may in fact be only a response to the community symbols with which they are identified.

It is hard to specify just which community symbols are

[19] E. L. Hartley and Ruth E. Hartley, *Fundamentals of Social Psychology* (New York, 1952); Robert F. Bales, "The Equilibrium Problem in Small Groups," in Talcott Parsons, Robert F. Bales, and Edward A. Shils, *Working Papers in the Theory of Action* (Glencoe, Ill., 1953).

[20] Duncan, *op. cit.*, p. 107.

identified with a particular figure, but news accounts, commentators, and the individual in question himself soon associate every prominent official's name and acts with a particular set of abstractions. J. Edgar Hoover is identified with patriotism, law enforcement, and security from subversion, all potent community symbols. Lyndon Johnson and the late Sam Rayburn presented themselves, and were constantly presented in the newspapers, as embodying the virtues of political compromise and brokership and representative government, symbols quite different from the ones that had been identified a generation earlier with another House Speaker, Joseph Cannon of Illinois. Cannon came to stand for something like authoritarian rule and legislative supremacy. The revealing point is that from the point of view of the general public these community symbols create different personalities for the best-known public officials. Nor are these necessarily misleading impressions. The Greeks assumed that only in the public realm could individuality be fully expressed and known. It was "the only place where men could show who they really and inexchangeably were." [21]

I have argued that leaders and the led provide essential psychological benefits for each other. The leader's dramaturgical jousts with public problems make the world understandable and convey the promise of collective accomplishment to masses who are bewildered, uncertain, and alone. A following and the premises conveyed through organization confer leadership and power upon incumbents of high office. In spite of these mutual supports the tie between a political leader and his following must remain a strained one. On both sides there are inevitable uncertainties and fears of betrayal. A review of some of the reasons and occasions for such anxieties makes a fitting close for this chapter, for in the last analysis leadership is always temporary and uneasy.

The most obvious occasion for mutual tension arises when either side explicitly denies that the tie between them exists. Leaders are constantly aware that their past success in capital-

---

[21] Arendt, *op. cit.*, p. 38.

izing upon followers' interests will not save them in the future if their dramatic performances become inadequate or the organizations upon which they rely for value and factual premises fail them. Their tenure as leaders may end for failure to follow their followers.

The leader who makes no effort to identify himself with approved community symbols or roles, but whose tenure is secure, thereby greatly increases public anxiety and irrationality. Men expect that leaders' acts will be rationalized as dealing with problems of general concern, even if there is no discernible payoff. An official or oligarchy that refuses to justify its actions is bound to make people wonder whether the problems they do not know how to handle themselves are being dealt with at all or whether some other grand design, benign or malevolent, motivates the leaders' acts. Fear and irrationality are the response to inexplicable and seemingly arbitrary acts.[22] Basically, however, this reaction stems from the expectation in all polities, even the most despotic, that rulers will avow that they are acting in the public interest.

A special case of this form of mass response often appeared in colonial states. Lucian Pye has generalized that "when not supported by other roles, the administrator may increase the psychic 'gap' between elite and mass."[23] Here the community symbols with which the colonial administrator invests his public personality are those with which the elite identifies, and they are therefore divisive.

A more general reason for anxiety lies in the circumstance that the political leader's role and identifications can seldom be clear-cut. This naturally requires the public to be consciously or subconsciously anxious as to whether the leader's posture and dramaturgical performance is a reliable indication of his ability and values: whether their public concerns are being managed with integrity. Because politics always in-

[22] *Ibid.*, p. 245.
[23] Lucian W. Pye, "Administrators, Agitators, and Brokers," *Public Opinion Quarterly*, Vol. 22 (Fall, 1958), p. 346.

volves social conflict, the successful politician must be ambivalent. There will always be a public sense of this fact no matter how unequivocal particular statements and actions may be. No observer can be sure in what circumstances Johnson or Goldwater will choose to represent a particular group's interests, though the odds may be clear enough; and he can be even less sure when either figure will let his ambivalence detract from his vigor in pursuing a policy line to which he is professedly committed. For the polity as a whole such ambivalence contributes to the representation of all group interests; but for each group and individual it makes for tension.

If uncertainty about a leader's intentions and his resolution is common, so is anxiety about the ultimate consequences of his acts, no matter how admirable his intentions may appear to be. I suggested early in this chapter that men's inability to foresee the consequences of acts is a central reason for their anxious acceptance of the leader's promises and of their consequent willingness to follow. Anxiety about ultimate consequences is not erased, however, but frequently renewed. Hannah Arendt declares: "They [men] have always known that he who acts never quite knows what he is doing, that he always becomes 'guilty' of consequences he never intended or even foresaw, that no matter how disastrous and unexpected the consequences of his deed he can never undo it, that the process he starts is never consummated unequivocally in one single deed or event, and that its very meaning never discloses itself to the actor but only to the backward glance of the historian who himself does not act."[24] Every citizen is personally exposed often enough to adverse unintended consequences of leaders' acts that his skepticism must become very profound, if not always overt. Policies put forward as remedies for recession do not get him back his job. A summit meeting hailed as establishing a new era of understanding is followed fairly quickly by a new crisis. A general's plan of attack brings a setback and the death of friends.

[24] Arendt, *op. cit.*, p. 209.

Ascription of leadership is profoundly a function of the passing of time. The leader as an historical figure is not the same symbol as he was to his contemporaries. Always, however, he is made to be what will serve the interests of those who follow him or write about him or remember him.

The creation of law and regularity and personal planning where accident, chaos, and impersonality are feared is his key symbolic function. We speak a great deal about our "government of laws and not of men," but we must write histories about culture heroes who established the laws and sustained them.

Leadership symbols may well be a more powerful factor in historical re-creation than in contemporary behavior. Roosevelt's lend-lease deal in 1940 reinforced the impression of his firm leadership at the time for both his supporters and his opponents; but it was then a highly controversial act, bringing charges of a sell-out of the nation's interests and of arbitrary, unconstitutional behavior. As time passes, the lend-lease agreement grows less controversial, coming to stand for effective leadership and correct judgment, for we read our knowledge of Pearl Harbor and a successful war back into it. The same is true of Theodore Roosevelt's anti-trust speeches and actions.

A historical figure generally identified with honored national symbols is especially useful to a group which can also associate him with its own interests. Jefferson serves the opponents of federal spending today better than Hoover. Leadership is re-created historically by writers and interest groups, as it is created contemporaneously by followers.

CHAPTER 5

Political Settings as Symbolism

Although every act takes place in a setting, we ordinarily take scenes for granted, focussing our attention on actions. When certain special kinds of acts are to take place, however, a very different practice prevails. Great pains are taken to call attention to settings and to present them conspicuously, as if the scene were expected either to call forth a response of its own or to heighten the response to the act it frames. Such accenting of settings typically accompanies theatrical performances, religious ceremonies, and the more common types of formal political actions.

Witnesses of political acts are likely to be sensitive to settings and to judge them as appropriate or inappropriate. The courtroom, the police station, the legislative chamber, the party convention hall, the presidential and even the mayoral office, the battleship or chamber in which the formal offer of surrender in war is accepted all have their distinctive and dramaturgical features, planned by the arrangers and actors in the event and expected by their audiences.

The occasional departure from what is appropriate only points up the centrality of setting to the political process. A motorist arrested in a small town for speeding should not be too surprised if he is escorted to a grocery store or other little shop where the local justice of the peace dispenses justice in shirtsleeves when he can get away from a customer. In this situation the motorist is at least as likely to be offended by the unaesthetic setting in which the wheels of government grind slowly as by his fine. A scene that is perfectly suitable for selling groceries becomes shocking when a formal governmental proceeding takes place in it.

That settings have a vital bearing upon actors, upon responses to acts, and especially upon the evocation of feeling and aesthetic reactions has always been fully recognized in the arts. In the drama, the opera, the ballet, in the display of paintings and in the performance of music setting is plotted and manipulated, just as it often is in the staging of governmental acts. The student of politics who wishes to analyze with some precision the bearing of settings upon the behavior of political elites and masses can probably learn even more from aesthetic theory than from anthropology and social psychology, though all of these make pertinent contributions.

The common element in the political settings mentioned here and in others that might have been mentioned is their contrived character. They are unabashedly built up to emphasize a departure from men's daily routine, a special or heroic quality in the proceedings they are to frame. Massiveness, ornateness, and formality are the most common notes struck in the design of these scenes, and they are presented upon a scale which focuses constant attention upon the difference between everyday life and the special occasion when one appears in court, in Congress, or at an event of historic significance.

We know something of the impact of the manifestly contrived setting, so designed as to make clear that it is framing a special performance and not ordinary life. Such backgrounds make for heightened sensitivity and easier conviction in onlookers, for the framed actions are taken on their own terms. They are not qualified by inconsistent facts in the environment. The creation of an artificial space or semblance thus sets the stage for a concentration of suggestions: of connotations, of emotions, and of authority. It is for this reason that Susanne Langer regards the creation of a sem-

96

blance as vital to all the arts.[1] Through the creation of an artificial space a particular set of impressions and responses can be intensified, serving to condense and organize a wide range of connotations, free of the irrelevancies, distractions, and qualifications of which everyday life mainly consists.

Although a political setting is too rarely a work of art, some of the same psychological and symbolic consequences can be made to operate. The conspicuousness with which a setting is presented for observation and special attention in any social situation defines the degree to which an audience is being injected into an artificial universe or semblance. The latter in turn makes easier the functioning of evocative, condensation symbolism, as just indicated, and involves a corresponding diversion of attention from cognitive and rational analysis and manipulation of the environment. As examples of the two symbolic poles involved in this contrast we might cite on the one hand tribal ceremonies in a contrived setting of masks, totems, and formal dance, and, on the other hand, a mathematician or theoretical physicist working in his rather disorderly office or den, or, for that matter, a primitive tribesman carefully building himself a canoe. In the last two instances setting is not noticed as a frame at all, while the nature of the job forces constant attention upon cognitive manipulation of the environment or of referential symbols so as to produce a desired result. In the first example attention is diverted from the immediate environment and focused upon abstractions that powerfully grip emotions. They do so not because there is a demonstrable tie to desired results, as in logical or mathematical manipulation, but precisely because there is no tie to consequences at all, no means of verification. People are therefore free to assure each other that the symbol means what they all passionately want it to mean: rain, fertility, a good crop, or another shared need. There is no danger that reality will prove them all wrong because they are not observing

[1] Langer, *Feeling and Form*, pp. 46–48.

reality; and if the future upsets their hopes, countermagic or a failure to comply rigidly with the prescribed ritual can be blamed. Social suggestion, not individual work and verification, becomes the stimulus of activity, and what is suggested is implicit in the setting. It compels attention, emotional release, and compliance because it promises to end a source of deep and common anxiety if there is profound and shared faith in the symbol, with every individual an instrument of the common interest rather than a cognitive and empirical manipulator of reality.

These background observations regarding the functions of settings, in art and in primitive social organization, help us understand the circumstances in which settings are conspicuously presented for attention in modern government. Setting, one notices, fades in and out of attention in intriguing correspondence with: (1) the importance of impressing a large audience, as distinct from the need to convince an individual through logical demonstration; (2) the intention of legitimizing a series of future acts (whose content is still unknown) and thereby maximizing the chance of acquiescence in them and of compliance with rules they embody; (3) the need to establish or reinforce a particular definition of the self in a public official. Comments already made bear upon the first of these functions of political settings, and other illustrations appear in the course of the chapter. The second and third functions are more specific, and each now calls for examination.

Kenneth Burke's insight that there is a rigid "ratio" between a dramatic setting and the quality of the acts that can take place within it and be regarded as appropriate offers a useful basis for the analysis of the tie between background and action. Several of his observations should be quoted:

It is a principle of drama that the nature of acts and agents should be consistent with the nature of the scene. . . .[2]
From the motivational point of view, there is implicit in the quality of a scene the quality of the action that is to take place

[2] Burke, *op. cit.*, p. 3.

within it. This would be another way of saying that the act will be consistent with the scene.[3]

. . . the stage-set contains the action *ambiguously* (as regards the norms of action) — and in the course of the play's development this ambiguity is converted into a corresponding articulacy. The proportion would be: scene is to act as implicit is to explicit. One could not deduce the details of the action from the details of the setting, but one could deduce the quality of the action from the quality of the setting.[4]

The appropriateness of act to setting is normally so carefully plotted in the political realm that we are rarely conscious of the importance or ramifications of the tie between the two. Burke's emphasis upon compatibility between the "quality" of acts and their settings naturally points toward the desirability of specifying concrete qualities if possible. Perhaps the most conspicuous kind of quality political scenes suggest is the emotional context of the acts they enfold. The judicial bench and chambers, formal, ornate, permanent and solid, lined with thick tomes, "prove" the deliberateness, scholarliness, and judiciousness of the acts that take place in them, even though careful study of some of these acts in a university or newspaper office (different settings) may indicate they were highly arbitrary, prejudiced, or casual. The severe, mobile setting of a military commander's camp in the field helps establish for the public his assertiveness, hardness, and self-assurance, as do the quality of his statements and communiques. Because the speeches are separable from tactics and are addressed to a different audience, they help establish the setting in this instance. When communiques embody craftsmanlike epitomes of the qualities we expect in a commander, they become memorable: "Nuts." "We have met the enemy and they are ours." "Veni, vidi, vici." Formality and ornateness in physical setting would be regarded here as evidence of incompetence, as would scholarliness or slow weighing of alternatives in action.

[3] *Ibid.*, pp. 6–7.
[4] *Ibid.*, p. 7.

That settings are addressed to different, wider audiences than acts is vital to the significance of the transaction. Burke's formulation rather obscures this distinction, but consideration of political acts and settings focuses attention upon it, and it confirms his main insight. The military commander's communiques and postures are addressed to the civilian population in his own country and perhaps in other countries, including the enemy's; but his troop deployments and bombardments are addressed to the bases of the enemy's military power, especially enemy troops. Judicial settings and dicta are addressed to all those whose confidence in the competence and judiciousness of the judicial system is important, but court decisions are addressed to litigants and to the accused. Setting helps legitimize an act for those who might oppose or overturn it politically by establishing that it was not properly or appropriately motivated.

Settings cannot, in fact, serve their function at all except as they are addressed to mass audiences rather than face-to-face, interacting groups. An especially revealing illustration of this fact can be found in the history of presidential press conferences over the last thirty years. Superficially, and as presented by White House press secretaries and most of the mass media, the trend has been steadily toward a closer rapport between the President and the people. Franklin Roosevelt held closed meetings with reporters, with direct quotation usually forbidden and much information labeled "background" and unpublishable. Eisenhower made much of his permission to record press conferences for later editing and broadcasting. Kennedy's Press Secretary claimed that his Chief moved even closer to the people by permitting live telecasts of press conferences.

When we apply to this trend our propositions about the psychological effects of settings, it becomes clear why the more perceptive observers and reporters have complained that the movement has in fact been in the direction of greater remoteness, less information, and far more contriving of impressions. The Roosevelt pattern permitted the

President to convey information, to set off trial balloons, and to be fully responsive to questions when he wished to be, precisely because he did not have to concern himself with mass impressions. Interaction and information, not setting, were emphasized. There was accordingly more news and more data and close contact with reporters, though the President had then to rely on other devices, such as the fireside chat, to address mass audiences.

The television screen, presenting a live performance, creates not close contact but a semblance of close contact, and the distinction is crucial. Though the picture is in one's living room, the President is remote and in a frame, and he is patently offering a performance. Unlike the Chief Executive engaging in an exchange with reporters alone, his words are now unchallengeable and unchangeable. The reporters asking questions are themselves part of the setting. Like every dramatic performance, this one concentrates impressions and evocations, becoming its own justification. Instead of a channel of information, we have an instrument for influencing opinion and response. The setting, and the mass audience to respond to it, define the situation and the action.

In general, then, the focussing of attention on settings is itself evidence either that there is a conscious effort to manipulate meanings and mass response or that the setting is inappropriate to the action. Our statements about act-setting ratios are specifications of what audiences will find acceptable or unacceptable. A difference in the quality of scene and act produces shock or anger or anxiety or a suspicion that the actor is incompetent. It therefore threatens his continued incumbency. The act is not legitimized. In the continuous interaction between official actor and mass public, setting supplies both the norms or justification for the action and the limits beyond which mass restiveness and disaffection become increasingly probable.

As Duncan puts it, there are no neutral scenes.[5] As soon as a setting becomes a conscious object of attention it sets

[5] Duncan, *op. cit.*, p. 96.

the stage for some general type of action, offering or reinforcing suggestions of its motivation. "Background" and
"ground" are both synonymous and complementary.

It is possible to distinguish between a static and a dynamic
political function of settings. The immediate setting of any
act is likely to be widely characterized at once as either appropriate or inappropriate. This is true because the act occurs as part of a wider spatial and temporal background
which makes one type of act and its immediate setting acceptable and other types unacceptable. Given the background of war a military leader is expected to fight, and his
immediate headquarters are expected in turn to be appropriate to the emotional qualities of aggressiveness. Given a
background of detente the military leader who makes aggressive statements becomes a center of controversy. He is
not now expected either to be in the field or to speak as
though he is, but rather to serve in a solid Pentagon building or university armory as an adjunct to peacetime social
and governmental activity.

In this sense scenes and acts both reinforce and motivate
each other and also are spatially and temporally dynamic.
The setting in its widest sense creates the perspective from
which mass audiences will view a challenge and thereby defines their response to it and the emotional aura which accompanies the response. No matter what the dynamics by
which a business-as-usual aura comes into being, it there-
after defines the various specific acts and settings which governmental organs will find politically acceptable. Except for
those immediately involved as participants, the general public of the 1920's was likely to see business as benign, the
times as prosperous, the future as rosy, and the serious farm
depression as not part of the scene. This wide background,
framing what was visible and what was good and moving, in
turn defined a Federal Trade Commission policy of encouragement of oligopoly and a presidential posture of laissez-
faire.

A pragmatic definition of political setting, then, must recognize it as whatever is background and remains over a period of time, limiting perception and response. It is more than land, buildings, and physical props. It includes any assumptions about basic causation or motivation that are generally accepted.

That the politically relevant setting is not merely physical but also social in character is fundamental to symbol formation. As already noted, physical setting and the acts occurring within it are commonly judged as appropriate or inappropriate to a wider spatial and temporal setting which men cue each other to understand and accept. Mead suggests a view of setting very like that defined in the last paragraph when he writes, "The unity of the environment is that of organization of the conditions for the solution of the problem."[6]

In this connection the attitude of the ancient Greeks toward legislation is especially in point. As Hannah Arendt reminds us, the Greeks did not see the lawmaker as a politician, but rather as one who had to do his work before political activity could begin. "He therefore was treated like any other craftsman or architect and could be called from abroad and commissioned without having to be a citizen, whereas the right . . . to engage in the numerous activities which eventually went on in the *polis*, was entirely restricted to citizens."[7]

The laws create a space in which to act. This outlook is very much in keeping with the propositions about legal language and statutes in Chapters 6 and 7 of this book. In adopting this view the Greeks recognized that to draft a law is not to reflect a public "will"; it is only through subsequent bargaining and administrative decision-making that values find some sort of realization in policy. To formulate a law is essentially a job of constructing a setting in the sense of building background assumptions and limits that will per-

[6] Anselm Strauss (ed.), *The Social Psychology of George Herbert Mead* (Chicago, 1934), p. 85.
[7] Arendt, *op. cit.*, pp. 173–174.

sist over time and influence the quality of political acts but not their content or direction. A statute may do this in several ways. It may state norms: either vague ones to which everyone will agree ("promote the public interest") or the norms of a controversial group which is thereby legitimized. It may define an ultimate objective toward which administrators or judges are to strive ("maintain high levels of employment"). It may even specify benefits or penalties in cardinal numbers or other very specific terms ($1.25 an hour minimum wage), while leaving to subsequent political interplay the determination of who is to be covered and who exempted. It often creates administrative agencies to act in the future, specifying in some form the mode of access various interests are to enjoy.[8]

All these acts of the statutory draftsman amount to a statement of the legitimate claims to recognition of various social groups. They are neither commands nor predictions of future action. They do, however, perform all the functions of settings in both their static and their dynamic senses.

The nature of the connection between setting and other influences upon action can be specified rather more fully, although further exploration of this relationship would be useful. Morris emphasizes the impossibility of action unless both a stimulus and a supporting environment are present: "the fact that behavior takes place within a supporting environment implies that the sign alone does not cause the response evoked, since the sign is merely one condition for a response-sequence in the given situation in which it is a sign. The dog upon hearing the buzzer does not seek food wherever it happens to be (though certain components of a food-response — such as salivation — may appear when the buzzer is heard). Only if a supporting environment is present will it seek food."[9]

---

[8] For a detailed consideration of the significance of statutory mandates, see Murray Edelman, "Interest Representation and Policy Choice in Labor Law Administration," *Labor Law Journal*, Vol. 9 (March, 1958), pp. 218–226.

[9] Morris, *op. cit.*, p. 15.

The analogue for public policy formation is clear. Unless an appropriate political setting has been created, legitimizing a set of values and a mode of access, a group interest cannot be expressed in policy no matter how strong or widespread it may be. A unilateral presidential creation of a Fair Employment Practices Commission without sanctioning legislation is grudgingly tolerated so long as a wartime setting offers some sanction, but is promptly scuttled when this supporting environment fades. Presidential appeals for price and wage restraint are viewed as arbitrary intervention into private matters and routinely ignored unless managements and unions are themselves divided and ambivalent. Political decisions overtly reached through bargaining are commonly regarded as unsanctioned by an acceptable setting and are therefore unpopular with mass publics and resisted by them unless otherwise rationalized. Administrative acts, such as the presidential illustrations just cited, are frequently regarded as incompatible with the larger legislative and constitutional setting in which they occur, even though they may reflect quite accurately the immediate administrative background.[10]

More common in recent American politics than a probing of the outer limits legitimized by settings is a predilection for staying so comfortably inside the limits that the main impression conveyed is one of craftsmanship in conforming to the prevailing political climate. Indeed, it has been clearly possible for presidents, majority leaders, and House speakers of the fifties and sixties to develop into an art the devising of public acts notable chiefly for their craftsmanlike conformity to the aura of the prevailing setting, but which are so trivial or inevitable that their major function is to preserve the leader's popularity. A leader who is regarded as the epitome of his times is necessarily an artful exponent of the quality of his setting. Such officials may sometimes arouse controversy, but this leadership style in-

[10] The group ties among bargaining, administration, and political settings are considered in more detail in Chapter 7.

volves careful rationing of controversial issues to a number sufficient to maintain the impression of aggressiveness if it is fashionable, while lavishing militancy almost entirely up- on issues for which it is not needed in the sense that the battle is already won.[11]

Only very rarely can a person perceive the whole of even a physical setting at one time, and it is manifestly impossible to perceive a social setting in its full spatial and temporal ex- tension. The question therefore arises how men, individually and collectively, normally take settings into account so that they may judge acts as compatible or incompatible with background. If the mechanism by which this is accomplished could operate only infrequently or under special conditions, then its influence upon political activity would be corre- spondingly limited.

Apparently, however, the mechanism is such that there is considerable opportunity for background to influence re- sponse to acts, for even a part of the setting evokes it. On this point Ogden and Richards say: "When a context has affected us in the past the recurrence of merely a part of the context will cause us to react in the same way in which we reacted before. A sign is always a stimulus similar to some part of an original stimulus and sufficient to call up an ex- citation similar to that caused by the original stimulus."[12]

There are many political applications of this principle. Lloyd Warner in his Yankee City study has given us exam- ples of the ability of condensation symbols to evoke again the intense emotional aura of a setting with which the sym- bol is associated and thereby to influence the political value structures of people. He documents the manner in which a Memorial Day celebration, for example, called up the sup- porting environment of America's wars and reawakened

[11] For further discussion of the phenomenon, see the discussion of symbolic leadership in Chapter 4.

[12] C. K. Ogden and I. A. Richards, *The Meaning of Meaning* (New York, 1952), p. 53.

some associations that had grown dim.[13] Alger Hiss has become associated for most Americans with the norms of the
thirties or those of the era dominated by Senator McCarthy,
and references to the Hiss case re-establish those settings. It
is especially significant that the evoked settings need not
have been physically experienced. Many Yankee City resi-
dents of the 1940's and 1950's had not lived through the wars
and the heroic era Memorial Day symbolized for them.
There is, in fact, some question whether this America ever
existed. The test of the political potency of a setting is a
consensus on its norms and on the effects attached to them
by a mass public, not the historical verifiability of the setting
or the accuracy of the consensual perception.

In view of these effects of settings upon values and behavior it is to be expected that the same political act may be
regarded as legitimate in one setting and shocking in another. Kenneth Burke offers a revealing illustration. He remarks
that businessmen despise "in the wrangles of the politicians, the reflection of the policies they as businessmen demand. So that they can admire the cause in themselves while
despising the symptom in their henchmen." While businessmen constantly praise their own commodity, "politicians
compete by slandering the opposition. When you add it all
up, you get a grand total of absolute praise for business and
a grand total of absolute slander for politics."[14] Notice, however, that the praise in the one situation and the slander in
the other are expected responses precisely because a higher
moral standard is expected in public affairs than in private
ones. Therefore an act that evokes a disapproving reaction
when a public official performs it is regarded as shrewd business tactics in a private setting. Resort to misleading or
meaningless rhetoric is differently evaluated in the two
realms especially commonly.

[13] W. Lloyd Warner, *The Living and the Dead* (New Haven, Conn.,
1959), Chap. 8.
[14] Kenneth Burke, *Attitudes Toward History* (New York, 1937), pp.
196–197.

We can also illustrate the point with narrower settings as the variables. Pritchett has nominated as "the most potent myth in American political life" the belief that the United States Supreme Court is a nonpolitical body.[15] Burke goes farther, declaring that the Court is the organ that comes closest in our democracy to possessing the attributes of patriarchalism.[16] Certainly, the Court, like the meeting of tribal elders or the sybil's cave, calls up an atmosphere in which some measure of suspension of individual criticism and considerable credibility are regarded as appropriate responses. This is at least relatively true, as compared to what is appropriate in response to legislative or congressional acts. The Court can accordingly pursue some policies which organs conventionally regarded as political cannot: declare school segregation illegal, for example, and uphold a great many of the civil and political rights of Communists. By the same token a political act viewed as directed against the Court, such as the 1937 Roosevelt plan for its enlargement, becomes symbolic parricide, while bills to rig the political make-up of legislative and administrative agencies are routinely viewed as quite conventional ploys in the political game.

Settings not only condition political acts. They mold the very personalities of the actors. As Sherif formulates it in a major text in social psychology: "the individual in any human grouping develops an ego which more or less reflects his social setting and which defines in a major way the very anchorages of his identity in relation to other persons, groups, institutions, etc. . . . disruption of these anchorages, or their loss, implies psychologically the breakdown of his identity. Such a disruption or loss of the individual's moorings is accompanied by anxiety or insecurity." [17] Markey, discussing nonreflective modes of action, declares: "Group situations are thus seen to present the social backgrounds and surround-

15 C. Herman Pritchett, *The Roosevelt Court* (New York, 1945), p. 4.
16 Burke, *Attitudes Toward History*, pp. 59–61.
17 Sherif, *An Outline of Social Psychology*, p. 105.

ings in which social influences, symbolic and nonsymbolic, direct and limit the kind of personality which may be developed." [18] We should expect, then, that a person's values, style of life and of political action, and expectations of others' roles would be shaped by his social setting, symbolic and nonsymbolic.

Certain elements of political self-definition influenced by social settings have been uniformly noticed by the writers on political psychology. Clearest, apparently, are the definition of the self as a participant in a stable, continuing order or as excluded from it (the feudal vassal and the modern displaced person are polar examples); as protected by prevailing institutions or as expendable (the big business entrepreneuer abroad and the army enlisted man); as elite or as nonelite.

There is good evidence that an urban-industrial setting promotes a sense of political effectiveness. Lane's summary of several studies of the question declares: "A sense of political effectiveness is likely to be increased by association with industry, unions, and the complexity of urban living; it is negatively related to rural life and its less dense constituencies and greater face-to-face contact with politicians." [19] Relatively isolated living is apparently the key variable here. It is the quality and frequency of one's contacts with other people that seems to matter, not one's objective ability to influence policy. To be a part of an organization viewed as potent is evidently to derive some feeling of effectiveness. Especially revealing is the finding that such association is more important than personal contact with politicians. If government is viewed as remote and not directly approachable, faith in a mediating organization rather than in personal effort is understandable.

Other evidence of the crucial function of settings in shaping people's basic orientations toward politics appears in socialization studies. Differences among adults in political

[18] John F. Markey, *The Symbolic Process and Its Integration in Children* (New York, 1928), p. 171.

[19] Lane, *op. cit.*, pp. 154–155.

participation and orientation and in authoritarian disposi-
tions quite clearly have their origin in part in childhood environment. The mother's educational level and such aspects
of the family situation as income level and urban or rural
background are especially influential. The adult behavior
pattern established in most complete form by childhood
setting is party affiliation because of the simplicity of the
symbols involved and the easy possibility of direct indoc-
trination.[20]

A challenging hypothesis of a more specific kind about the
relationship between family background and party identification has been offered by a psychiatrist:

It is quite apparent that our political party affiliations are highly
emotionally surcharged loyalties and that we often tend to perceive one party as hero and the other as villain; one as succorant
and giving, the other retentive and refusing; one interested in
the "common man," the other the instrumentality of "special
interests." If the primary identifications are prototypic of the
secondary one, the needs and wishes which were unfilled in childhood are irrationally transferred to the political party of our
choice. We would then expect that a conflict between the maternal
and paternal images in childhood would result in the conflict
of voting choice.[21]

A significant difference in scope appears, then, between the
settings that influence political acts and those that shape the
self and its responses to political events and institutions.
Political acts must be compatible with settings physically or
symbolically expressive of particular *political* norms, legitimations, or postures. In identifying the backgrounds that
shape personality, however, we turn chiefly to *nonpolitical*
settings: to occupation, urban or rural character of the individual's surroundings, and family background. In the first
instance we are explaining how mass publics as audiences

20 Herbert Hyman, *Political Socialization* (Glencoe, Ill., 1959), p. 47.
21 C. W. Wahl in Eugene Burdick and Arthur J. Brodbeck, *American Voting Behavior* (Glencoe, Ill., 1959), p. 272.

view compatibility between act and scene. In the second instance we are explaining how people from particular demographic backgrounds mold themselves and hence their political gestures through the choice of significant others, whose roles they take.

If people's backgrounds are this important in shaping their values and responses, backgrounds have the most serious implications for policy formation. Patterns of social stratification, urbanization, industrialization, and authoritarian family behavior place severe limits upon the range of policies that will be popular or accepted. This factor must be considered, however, in conjunction with other symbolic interactions. It is often necessary for officials to overcome the limitations upon their maneuverability imposed by popular reactions through resort to legitimizing symbols. A government can neutralize a large part of its own population insistent upon a disarmament treaty by specifying as a prerequisite to disarmament seemingly reasonable conditions known in advance to be unacceptable to other countries involved in the negotiations: an inspection requirement, for example. Opponents of nuclear testing in the atmosphere can be mollified by repeated references to past testing or to plans for future testing by a potential enemy country.

One type of setting especially common in the political process stems directly from the inevitable prevalence in government of large bureaucracies. For reasons reviewed in the chapters on administrative symbolism large numbers of people asking benefits, favors, or what they regard as their rights from governmental bureaucracies are denied what they seek. Taking the roles of specific clienteles, bureaucratic organizations frequently are not responsive to larger and less well organized publics. Some of the reasons this lack of responsiveness is not more generally resented or protested are analyzed elsewhere; but setting often plays a significant part as well by creating an atmosphere that is forbidding and difficult to penetrate.

In some degree the forbidding aspect of the setting is physical. The long corridors, closed doors, unfamiliar bureau and section names, and succession of subordinates serving as screens to the presence of officials can create a Kafkaesque aura. As in *The Trial* and *The Castle* the atmosphere at once encourages timidity in the outsider seeking favors and foreshadows rebuffs from the insiders.

The petty bureaucrat, who more often than his superiors comes into direct contact with the unorganized clientele, is prone to complement the advantage offered by his physical setting with the invocation of an even more forbidding social setting symbolized in "the rules." These are unseen and untouchable and hence, like all dogma, not to be violated, altered, or questioned. Their invocation is a signal that discussion of the merits of the issue is out of place and profane, that what is involved is the transmission and conservation of a sacred tradition.[22] Reference to "the rules" therefore evokes a symbolic political setting that is extremely confining with respect to appropriate action and behavior on both sides.

The shaping of the self or personality is also involved. Petty bureaucrats (including policemen) are especially likely to behave dogmatically when anxious about defiance from clients or reversal or sanctions from hierarchical superiors.[23] The rules then serve them as legitimation of their inflexible behavior.

This frequently encountered political situation, while only one type of example, serves as an apt summary of my major observations about settings. Individual claimants of benefits or favors and minor bureaucrats interact in the course of a long-standing pattern of behavior that ties policy to the interests of organized clientele groups. This larger temporal setting finds its immediate expression in a forbidding physical scene and in acts and speeches that evoke an untouchable

[22] Cf. Malinowski, *op. cit.*, pp. 48–49.

[23] For several analyses of the dynamics of this phenomenon by organizational theorists, see James G. March and Herbert A. Simon, *op. cit.*, pp. 36–47.

and emotionally compelling "semblance" characterized by dogmatism and restriction. Thus do various conceptual and physical echelons of settings and acts fit into and complement each other; the entire background shapes personalities able to engage indefinitely in the type of inflexible behavior that is politically and symbolically appropriate.

CHAPTER 6

Language and the Perception of Politics

1

If politics is concerned with who gets what, or with the authoritative allocation of values, one may be pardoned for wondering why it need involve so much talk. An individual or group can most directly get what it wants by taking it or by force and can get nothing directly by talk. The obvious difficulty is the possibility of resistance, and it is counterforce that talk may circumvent.[1]

The employment of language to sanctify action is exactly what makes politics different from other methods of allocating values. Through language a group can not only achieve an immediate result but also win the acquiescence of those whose lasting support is needed. More than that, it is the talk and the response to it that measures political potency, not the amount of force that is exerted. Force signals weakness in politics, as rape does in sex. Talk, on the other hand, involves a competitive exchange of symbols, referential and evocative, through which values are shared and assigned and coexistence attained. It is fair enough to complain that the politician is not deft in his talk, but to complain that he talks is to miss the point.

That talk is powerful is not due to any potency in words

[1] See Arendt, *op. cit.*, p. 159, for an elaboration of this theme.

but to needs and emotions in men. In subtle and obvious ways cultures shape vocabulary and meaning, and men respond to verbal cues. People who share the same role learn to respond in common fashion to particular signs. Specify a role and a political speech, and you can also specify a response with a high measure of confidence: the response of a labor union officer to the public official's declaration that wage increases must be restrained this year; the response of a Farm Bureau official to an argument that the government should guarantee a minimum income to farmers; the response of a Defense Department official to the argument that high military budgets and preparedness promote peace.

Meaning and response, then, are not the same for everyone, but a function of group interest or mutual role-taking. Pool has suggested how the meanings of symbols may be defined operationally: "A social scientist may define the meaning of a symbol to a given person as the sum of the contexts in which that person will use that symbol. The usages need not be consistent or 'proper,' but insofar as the usages occur in predictable contexts the symbol has meaning for the man who uses it and that meaning is an important fact to the social scientist." [2]

To the political scientist patterning or consistency in the contexts in which specific groups of individuals use symbols is crucial, for only through such patterning do common political meanings and claims arise. Morris declares: "the accurate description of a situation does not necessarily lead to a common preference by various interpreters or to common actions which are needed and which signs are used to effect. Hence the basic importance of signs which in themselves have appraisive and prescriptive signification common to members of a group. . . ." [3] Accuracy is not the important characteristic of political language, but the appraisals common to members of a group.

[2] Ithiel de Sola Pool, "Symbols, Meanings, and Social Science," in Lyman Bryson and others (eds.), *Symbols and Values: An Initial Study* (New York, 1954), Chap. 23.

[3] Morris, *op. cit.*, p. 117.

In the creation and spreading of appraisals, affect and emotion become part of the meaning of signs. Physicians exposed to the phrase "compulsory health insurance" react not to the dictionary definitions of three words but to a powerful set of economic and moral anxieties. Language becomes a sequence of Pavlovian cues rather than an instrument for reasoning and analysis if situation and appropriate cue occur together.

A mutual cuing within a group of evocative connotations may establish an aura around a sign, so that intensity is lent to the response. A word or phrase which has become established as connoting threat or reassurance for a group thus can become a cue for the releases of energy "out of all proportion to the apparent triviality of meaning suggested by its mere form." [4] The word is not in itself the cause; but it can evoke everything about the group situation that lends emotion to its political interests, abstracting, reifying, and magnifying. That a term masquerades as description while appraising and condensing doubtless heightens its emotional impact.

The cues can intensively placate and mollify as well as arouse, as numerous examples already cited illustrate. Indeed, the most commonly used and most abstract terms are, naturally enough, those that reassure the anxious that the "public interest" or the "national security" or the "national health and safety" are being protected. The words mean different specific things to different groups, and for that reason are generally efficacious.

The very structure of language contributes to such effects in subtle ways of which we are quite unconscious as we employ them and react to them. Izutsu points out, for example, that "this process of reification is greatly helped by the very natural tendency common to many languages . . . to express whatever becomes the subject of a verb in the form of a 'noun.' " [5] He cites fire, really a process, as something we express as if it were a substance. In politics we indulge in the

---

[4] Sapir, *op. cit.*, pp. 492–493.
[5] Toshihiko Izutsu, *Language and Magic* (Tokyo, 1956), p. 94.

same usage with words like "communism," "tyranny," and the "general welfare," conveying to others and to ourselves the assumption that there is a specific, commonly understood entity to be defended or fought through action or through suffering deprivation, and we use them as the subjects of verbs. Whatever diverse pictures may be in the minds of the various respondents to such cues, it is their action or their acquiescence in deprivation that is politically significant.

As a consequence of this interweaving of words and behavior, language is a necessary catalyst of politics, concentrating affect for groups seeking political favors and helping spectators of politics to abstract reassurances from a complex environment. Because the state is so potent and obsessive a symbol, arousal and emotional engagement are inevitable. Language interweaves with action so as to pattern the political behavior of aroused men into a viable and self-regulating system.

Because language is so efficient a tool for reifying the abstract, it is central to the practice endemic in contemporary culture of dealing in abstractions. They are often quantitative abstractions, lent prestige by the successes of science and by the preoccupation of business with profit and loss statements. They are often qualitative abstractions, such as the normative terms that permeate statutes and political exhortation. In either case they encourage men to focus their attention and their passions upon the remote and the symbolic and to move away from personal regard for quality and for creative work. They thereby magnify the possibility of manipulating people through manipulation of the symbols that engage them.

Max Weber has called attention to a vital political application of this phenomenon in his distinction between rational and empirical justice. Rational justice is "the interpretation of law on the basis of strictly formal conceptions" and empirical justice consists of "informal judgments rendered in terms of concrete ethical or practical valuations." The judge who relies upon precedent and codified legal principle exemplifies rational justice; the Mohammedan Kadi who hears the pleas of disputants and renders judgment for one or the other on the spot applies empirical justice.

In the first case the decision is rationalized in the abstract concepts of a legal code while the second "knows no reasoned judgment whatever." The first, Weber shows, serves the interest of the propertied groups, for the rational legal abstractions instrumentally emphasize property interests and also rationalize this emphasis. Empirical justice works more consistently in the interests of the poor, for attention is focussed upon their concrete needs and deprivations. "The propertyless masses especially are not served by a formal 'equality before the law' and a 'calculable' adjudication and administration, as demanded by 'bourgeois interests.' "[6] Essentially the same principle is often at work in contemporary political conflict between political machines and good government groups, the latter favoring rational law and administration and the former distributing favors on the basis of empirical claims. In a study of public housing policy and politics in Chicago, Meyerson and Banfield concluded that the political machine was consistently more favorable to the interests of those with relatively low incomes than the "reform" groups working for efficient, rationalized, and businesslike procedures in government.[7]

One form of abstraction that has grown in importance in recent decades is the counting of people's political wants. The spectators of politics are told several times a week which officeholders and candidates they like and how they stand on issues. Candidates for major office pay pollsters large sums of money to give them true pitch. Though neither candidates nor legislators nor voters are always swayed by the modern sybils, the great demand for their product offers a rough measure of our confidence in it.

To reduce ambivalent, subtle, interacting, contingent re-

[6] Gerth and Mills, *op. cit.*, pp. 216–221.

[7] Martin Meyerson and Edward Banfield, *Politics, Planning and the Public Interest* (Glencoe, Ill., 1955), Chap. 11.

sponses to statistics is to abstract and simplify grossly but not randomly. It is to describe the responses that occur given existing circumstances, a useful enough enterprise. It is to ignore or discount *possibilities* and the response to changed perspectives that political acts might themselves create if the actors were less bemused by popularity polls. It is therefore to exert a conservative influence in the degree that the statistics affect political activity. In the opinion polls we have an instrument that extends the legitimizing function of vote counting to a larger segment of the political process.[8]

It should be emphasized that there is nothing about abstraction in itself that requires stereotyped or rigid thinking. This response occurs only when an abstract term becomes a condensation symbol and takes on compelling connotations. Analysis inevitably involves abstraction; but here the analyst avoids affect or stereotyping by regarding his abstractions as fictions rather than truths or hypotheses. The neo-Kantian philosopher Vaihinger called attention early in this century to the pervasive use of fictions in all branches of science as a necessary aid to analysis and creative thinking. Discussing the uses of abstractions regarded as fiction he said, "This generalization breaks up the very constituents of existence and puts them together again in a far more general manner, in the process discovering the many possibilities which might still have been possible. Then the laws of *compossibilitas* (in the sense of Leibniz) are studied and the particular is thus more profoundly understood. . . . The great reformers of social life always think what exists as a special case among many possibilities."[9]

Only in the conscious analytic and synthetic employment of language to perceive new possibilities, however, do its terms become efficient tools, relatively free of the contagion of values. Virtually every word and phrase used in casual

[8] For a stimulating, if perhaps overdrawn, discussion of this theme see C. Wright Mills, *The Sociological Imagination* (New York, 1959), Chap. 3.

[9] Hans Vaihinger, *The Philosophy of "As If"* (London and New York, 1924), p. 55.

speech and thought bears a heavy connotative burden which opens the way to socially approved conclusions and inhibits the recognition of possibilities that are not culturally condoned. One of the more exciting linguistic discoveries of the past half-century is the recognition that every culture discloses and guides its system of values and its general perceptions in its language. For some areas of discourse a large number of words with fine shadings of meaning are available, permitting and encouraging careful distinctions and descriptions. In other areas a language may be quite barren, reflecting a lack of interest or a tabu and making inquiry difficult or impossible. Sapir calls attention to the fact that, "Distinctions which seem inevitable to us may be utterly ignored in languages which reflect an entirely different type of culture, while these in turn insist on distinctions which are all but unintelligible to us. . . . It would be difficult in some languages . . . to express the distinction which we feel between 'to kill' and 'to murder,' for the simple reason that the underlying legal philosophy which determines our use of these words does not seem natural to all societies."[10]

Both the perception of fact and value connotations hinge on the adequacy and character of the available vocabulary. This factor raises obstacles to innovation and encourages decision-making organizations to take the roles of well-established groups, a phenomenon described from another perspective in earlier chapters. It should help explain variation in public policy in diverse contemporary and past cultures.

Especially potent in influencing value premises is the circumstance that every society's vocabulary reflects many past beliefs and values still attracting attention and evoking responses. "The various structural peculiarities of a modern, civilized language carry . . . an enormous dead weight of archaic use, of magical superstition and of mystical vagueness,"

[10] Sapir, *op. cit.*, p. 36. See also Benjamin L. Whorf, "Science and Linguistics," in Sol Saporta (ed.), *Psycholinguistics* (New York, 1961), pp. 460–468.

Malinowski asserts,[11] and his finding is supported by the work of other reputable linguists.[12]

The magical associations permeating language are important for political behavior because they lend authoritativeness to conventional perceptions and value premises and make it difficult or impossible to perceive alternative possibilities. Izutsu observes: "The normative and authoritative nature of the language of law and the language of ethics cannot satisfactorily be explained if we leave out of account the magical contexts out of which they arose and with which they remain most closely connected." [13] And again, "what is involved in our use of even the most commonplace and ordinary general words, such as dog, cat, and house, is, as far as its connotative aspect goes, essentially the same as what was observed in the magical processes of invocation. . . ."[14] Formally also the same but connotatively much richer are the terms in which governmental actions and procedures are described and evaluated: court, law, crime, election, hearing, writ. By evoking emotional associations they lend intensity to belief and espousal, and they may also get in the way of criticism and rational manipulation, a process that is discussed below.

The words a group employs and on which it relies to evoke a response can often be taken as an index of group norms and conceptual frameworks. The word "freedom," as of the early 1960's, seems to be favored by the bureaucracies of patriotic and veterans organizations and of the armed services and by others taking similar roles, often in the course of rationalizing authority, nationalist gestures, or deprivation. As a polar example, an Air Force public relations officer has met criticisms of the damage to property wrought by planes

[11] Malinowski, "The Problem of Meaning in Primitive Languages," in C. K. Ogden and I. A. Richards, *The Meaning of Meaning* (New York, 1959), p. 265.

[12] Cf. Izutsu, *op. cit.*, Chap. 4; Sapir, *op. cit.*, pp. 35–36. See also Harold Lasswell, "Key Symbols, Signs, and Icons," in Lyman Bryson, Louis Finkelstein, R. M. MacIver, and Richard McKean (eds.), *Symbols and Values: An Initial Study* (New York and London, 1954), p. 201.

[13] Izutsu, *op. cit.*, p. 38.

[14] *Ibid.*, p. 60.

breaking the sound barrier by suggesting that the ear-splitting reverberation of the planes be publicized as "the sound of freedom." The word "liberty," on the other hand, is apparently preferred by groups espousing individual freedom from state control and deprivation, as in "civil liberty." At the time of the Revolutionary War "liberty" evidently aroused some of the connotations "freedom" does today, and so we have the "liberty bell." We are sufficiently conditioned to the current usages that each word serves as a cue for the appropriate set of norms, though usually not consciously so. It evokes a rationalization for a particular kind of behavior and an argument against another kind.

The terms "social welfare" and "charity" similarly serve as indexes to subcultures and to differences in norms and in historical depth.

These examples presumably illustrate part of what Lasswell had in mind when he wrote: "it is apparent that *change in the spread and frequency of exposure* to key signs is an exceedingly significant indicator of important social processes. We can follow the dissemination of secular or sacred cults by surveying trends in the geographical distribution of icons and other significant signs found in the whole complex. Similarly, we can establish the presumption of integrative or disintegrative trends within any society by observing sign frequencies."[15]

Signs evoke an intense response only for those already taking the roles that make them sensitive to the cues that are given off. To describe the aid to dependent children program as "charity" may arouse an unfavorable reaction toward the program in some people, while in others it arouses an unfavorable reaction toward the speaker. If we know in which of these ways a person responds, we can predict quite confidently how he will respond to the term "social welfare."

Lazarsfeld and his associates concluded from their voting behavior studies that propagandistic language used in the course of election campaigns serves chiefly to arouse voting

[15] Lasswell, "Key Symbols, Signs, and Icons," p. 201.

predispositions rather than to change voting intentions or behavior.[16] This finding is also consistent with the view that linguistic cues serve chiefly to provide motive force for incipient gestures rather than to change the gestures.

Practical politicians usually recognize the emptiness of hortatory rhetoric that tries to activate interests other than those rooted in the material situation of the audience. Lobbyists relying on such rhetoric get short shrift.

Congressmen, for example, are skeptical about labor spokesmen or the League of Women Voters when they use lofty arguments about issues in which their membership has no immediate economic interest.[17] A great deal of casual political discussion and of formal political oratory consists of such rhetoric. The politician's hard-headed skepticism therefore serves to insulate a high proportion of the expressive political verbalizing that takes place from meshing directly with decision-making processes or even with symbol creation in legislative bodies.

This view of propaganda has some interesting corollaries. Political argument, when it is effective, calls the attention of a group with shared interests to those aspects of their situation which make an argued-for line of action seem consistent with the furthering of their interests. It is an effort to speed up a process of "thinking" which takes place at some pace anyway. There are, however, limits to its persuasive power in the feedback between men's situations and their perceptions.

It is possible to formulate a more specific hypothesis on this subject: that material benefits that are directly and immediately forthcoming encourage political rhetoric in line with object appraisal; and that perception of threat encourages rhetoric that externalizes tension. Men are often in political situations in which the two tendencies oppose each other, and the hypothesis often permits explanation or prediction of action because for a specific group one or the other

16 Lazarsfeld, Berelson, and Gaudet, *op. cit.*, Chap. 8.
17 Lane, *op. cit.*, pp. 66–67.

interest is the more immediate. The officers of the AFL-CIO, in lobbying for a civil rights bill and liberal tariff policies, get some immediate status benefit from posing as statesmen influential in the general affairs of state. The rank-and-file members do not share in this benefit, are likely to find the objectives of such legislation remote from their experience, and sometimes find that they clash with perceptions of immediate interests: economic or status rivalry with Negroes or employment in an industry losing its market to foreign goods. Congressmen who ignore the official labor position on civil rights or foreign trade can accordingly be fairly confident that the votes and the lofty rhetoric will often be found in different places.

The propagandist whose verbalizations are most intensely embraced is the one who finds a formulation that evokes and synthesizes a large number of the experiences of concern to his audience. Semantically, and even phonetically, words and phrases have rich associations unless they are deliberately divested of them by an analyst who fits terms into a narrow and clear scheme. This is useful for logic but can be fatal to propaganda. "The symbols of the over-schematized propagandist are thin," Burke declares, "more like the symbols of a filing system than the symbols of the 'linguistic dance.'"[18]

II

These are some of the functions of language in shaping and catalyzing perception and behavior. Language sometimes directly encourages behavior contrary to people's interests, and we can specify at least some of the processes that are involved.

One of them is the employment of political speech and writing as a ritual, dulling the critical faculties rather than awakening them. Chronic repetition of clichés and stale phrases that serve simply to evoke a conditioned uncritical response is a time-honored habit among politicians and a mentally restful one for their audiences. The only informa-

[18] Burke, *Attitudes Toward History*, p. 110.

tion conveyed by a speaker who tells an audience of businessmen that taxes are too high and that public spending is waste is that he is trying to prevent both himself and his audience from thinking and to make all present join in a favored liturgy consisting of the ritualistic denunciation of the symbols "taxes" and "spending." In an essay devoted to the proposition that "political writing is bad writing," George Orwell remarks: "If the speech he [a politician] is making is one that he is accustomed to make over and over again, he may be almost unconscious of what he is saying, as one is when one utters the responses in church. And this reduced state of consciousness, if not indispensable, is at any rate favorable to political conformity." [19]

Such mutual supplying of inartistic gratifications by speaker and audience can become a hazard to rational action because it can prevent systematic analysis of one's situation and interests. Phrases and the acts they name become invested with narcissism,[20] so that men support or oppose as a conditioned response whatever is accepted in their group as "American," as "segregation," as "socialized medicine," or as "standing up to Krushchev." The term is no longer recognized as a symbol but is considered a primary goal; and to discuss it, praise it, denounce it, or repeat it becomes a real gratification.[21]

Once a term becomes a vehicle for expressing a group interest it goes without saying that it is in no sense descriptive, but only evocative. When one man speaks of "governmental control" and "private enterprise" and another of "private control" and "government enterprise," we learn nothing from their speech about political economy but we do learn something important about the group values with which each identifies.[22]

We cannot erase the problem simply by being careful in

[19] George Orwell, "Politics and the English Language," in *A Collection of Essays* (New York, 1954), p. 172.

[20] Cf. Lasswell, *Psychopathology and Politics*, p. 195.

[21] Karl Mannheim, *Man and Society* (New York, 1941), p. 132.

[22] Rupert Crawshay-Williams, *The Comforts of Unreason* (London, 1947), p. 72.

the use of words, for it is rooted in social role-taking, not in individual carelessness. Furthermore, not naming can be as lethal to rational action as misnaming. We constantly go on doing things, often very efficiently, which need not be done at all or which prevent the achievement of goals. They are not questioned because they are not named. Throughways and freeways are associated with speed, and we run them into the central portions of large cities. In the minds of their political supporters they facilitate speedy access to downtown areas, but on many roads every morning and evening they offer much slower transportation to commuters than public trains can offer, and congestion is getting steadily worse. In 1911 a horse-drawn vehicle in New York City averaged 11½ miles an hour, but the average speed of automobiles in the city today is about six miles an hour.[23] To give the problem explicit verbalization is to question it and begin to look for a solution; for those who name the freeways rather than the problem there is little reasoning.[24]

Syntax and the prevailing sign structure thus implicitly express the ideology of the community, facilitate uncritical acceptance of conventional assumptions, and impede the expression of critical or heretical ideas. A system of signs that objectively hurts a group can even be embraced and protected by the group it injures. Morris offers a careful description of the phenomenon:

If . . . the power of the community has fallen into the hands of a group of persons who exploit the community for their own ends, the success of this group in prohibiting changes in the sign structure of the society which would be disadvantageous to its members is not a matter of sign pathology; it is with respect to such persons an adequate use of signs. Judged from the standpoint of society it is immoral and inadequate, but still not pathic. Suppose, however, that the people themselves who are thus exploited, and as a social group, actively resist change in the very sign structure by

23 Lewis Mumford, *The City in History* (New York, 1961), pp. 503–509.
24 For further consideration of the social consequences of not naming, see Burke, *Attitudes Toward History*, p. 70.

which they are exploited, then the situation would have become socially pathic. The signs in question may relieve certain anxieties in the members of society with respect to the social behavior in which they are engaged, and so be cherished for this satisfaction even though the signs hinder or even make impossible the actual realization of the goals of such social behavior itself. . . . Signs then become socially pathic only insofar as a number of persons constituting a society resist changes in the correction of signs which function in the social behavior of this group because of the partial satisfaction these signs give to such social behavior.[25]

We can be more specific about the political satisfactions such a pathic sign structure conveys to those who use and embrace it. It makes their polity meaningful and it gives them status. These are values for which men fight hard. The rebel who assures liberals that the reform legislation which gives them their reason for being liberals is a sham can expect severe resistance and not gratitude, and he can anticipate the same reaction from conservatives, whose world he just as fundamentally undermines. It is the conventional responses to such words as "liberal," "conservative," "regulation," and "law" that constitute the prevailing political sign structure, providing an order that permits groups to act, to anticipate the responses of others, and to acquire status. To suggest that the signs around which all this group interplay revolves are misleading is to threaten chaos and to arouse opposition. In the existing order the elite can gain both the material and the symbolic rewards of politics through defense of the prevailing sign structure, while other groups are unable to achieve both forms of benefit through any single course of action.

Rebellion is itself an ambivalent response to signs to which most of the population responds conventionally. It cannot be understood simply as reflecting the rebel's perception of incompatibility between his material situation and the connotations of the prevailing sign structure. Such incompatibility is manifestly so common that rebellion would

[25] Morris, *op. cit.*, pp. 210–211.

be constant and endemic if it depended on any such simple basis. Rebellion has, moreover, consistently occurred after material conditions had begun to improve and not when they were at their worst.[26] If the improvement in conditions is planned by the elite, it may be taken as evidence that the prevailing sign structure, embodying an ideology that rationalizes deprivation and assumes its inevitability, has begun to be questioned. If, as is more likely, the improvement accompanies unplanned social and economic changes, it brings at least some of the deprived population an awareness of the possibility of higher living standards and also brings contacts with ideologies that supply rationalizations of higher standards. The unconventional response may, alternatively, have its basis in the rebels having been reared in a marginal class, economic, ethnic, or nationalistic milieu. In any case terms connoting new possibilities have become part of the rebels' sign structure, and there is in consequence an ambivalent response to the established structure.[27]

Unconventional response to signs connoting authority is politically important only when it attracts a following and is therefore relatively widespread. Rebellion cannot depend, as the elite are fond of asserting, on the neurotic or psychotic state of a rebel leader. Without a following he is a crank or a crackpot. That he has a following does not necessarily mean that the rebels' response is rational or will bring them material benefits, but it does mean that for them the kind of pathic response Morris analyzes has not occurred.

Rebellion, however, is to be understood as an exceptional event, useful here to clarify the customary function of a sign structure. Typically, in Lasswell's words, *"Key signs provide a unifying experience* fostering sentiments that may transcend limitations of culture, class, organization, and personality."[28]

[26] Crane Brinton, *The Anatomy of Revolution* (New York, 1938).
[27] Morris, *op. cit.*, p. 202. For some related propositions about the occasions of rebellion, see Chapter 8.
[28] Harold Lasswell, "Key Symbols, Signs and Icons," p. 201.

One sense in which key signs unify is through so shaping the perception of experience as to still or minimize discontent. This book has suggested many examples, and will cite others, of the manner in which myth, ritual, settings, leaders' actions, and language promote quiescence. These symbolic forms serve to reconcile belief-systems with behavior, stretching one or the other in the interest of social and political viability. We see symbolism in this light best in alien cultures, where we are not involved in the prevailing belief-systems and therefore scrutinize institutions rather than accept them. In the course of a discussion of legal fictions, Max Weber offers a neat example of the symbolic stretching of a belief-system to justify necessary economic activity: "The rigorous sectarianism of the Shiites . . . would have prohibited as unclean all economic intercourse with nonbelievers. But through a number of fictions this sectarianism claimed by sacred law has ultimately been almost completely renunciated." [29]

As human beings can function in society, and hence as men, only through such continuous reconciliation of what is required of them physically or bureaucratically and what is required of them symbolically, it is to be expected that the signs for accomplishing the reconciliation will be powerful ones. While the content of sign structures differ, they are alike in requiring man to identify himself with something perceived as guiding his course: the right, the true, the inevitable. Thereby his dubious acts are sanctified and his responsibility as an individual entity minimized. The constitution, the laws of nature, reason, or other potent symbols justify man's lot and his acts; and they are invoked not only explicitly but also implicitly through the structure of language.

[29] Max Rheinstein (ed.), *Weber, on Law in Economy and Society* (Cambridge, Mass., 1954), p. 243.

CHAPTER 7

The Forms and Meanings
of Political Language

1

This chapter identifies several distinctive language styles that pervade and characterize the political process and examines the manner in which they facilitate the resolution of group conflict.

Language, we are told by the linguists, anthropologists, and social psychologists who have studied it, is not to be conceived as something which conveys meaning by itself. Its meanings are always a function of the context from which it issues, of the disparate needs and interests of the audiences involved, and of their respective modes of perception.[1] The realistic study of political language and its meanings is necessarily a probing not only of dictionaries, nor of word counts, but of the diverse responses to particular modes of expression of audiences in disparate social settings. For politics is in one sense a drama played simultaneously by and before many audiences in many different social settings. Some elements are relatively stable and others highly dy-

[1] For accounts of the relation between verbal and nonverbal behavior, see the following studies: Clyde Kluckhohn, *Mirror for Man* (New York, 1959); Kenneth L. Pike, *Language in Relation to a Unified Theory of the Structure of Human Behavior, Part I*, Preliminary Edition (Glendale, Calif., 1954), Chap. 1; Izutsu, *op. cit.*, especially Chap. 10. Bronislaw Malinowski, "The Problem of Meaning in Primitive Languages," in Ogden and Richards, *op. cit.*, pp. 306–336.

namic, changing quickly with the public issue, the conspicuous actors, the dominant domestic and foreign threat, and so on; and the changes influence the meaning of the speeches. To hear the sentence, "Castro is a Socialist," spoken over the radio is to have little clue to its meaning if one does not know, among other things, whether Khrushchev, Adlai Stevenson, Robert Welch, or Norman Thomas is speaking, whether we are currently in a period of international tension or detente, and whether the program is beamed to Russia or North America.

Dewey and Bentley have declared that naming may usefully be viewed "as itself directly a form of knowing." [2] The terms in which we name or speak of anything do more than designate it; they place it in a class of objects, thereby suggest with what it is to be judged and compared, and define the perspective from which it will be viewed and evaluated. To speak of picketing as a form of expression is to know it as one kind of thing and associate it with a quite definite class of objects and evaluations; to speak of it as a form of pressure is to know it as a quite different thing, in a different universe of objects, differently evaluated. Language is not just one more kind of activity; it is, in the sense just discussed, the key to the universe of speaker and audience. Many students of cultural anthropology, logic, and social psychology have demonstrated that this function of language is no ephemeral influence, but the central factor in social relations and action.[3] It is all the more potent because it operates unconsciously for the most part, permeating perception, conception, and experience.

This chapter deals in the main with those meanings of political language associated with its forms or styles. These are both more persistent and stable than the connotations of

[2] John Dewey and Arthur F. Bentley, *Knowing and the Known* (Boston, reprint 1960), p. 147.

[3] Edward Sapir, *Culture, Language, and Personality* (Berkeley and Los Angeles, 1960); Anselm L. Strauss, *Mirrors and Masks* (Glencoe, Ill., 1959), Chap. 1; O. Hobart Mowrer, *Learning Theory and Symbolic Behavior* (New York, 1959), Chap. 4.

the content of language, and also more subtle. Most of the time we are not at all aware that meanings are conveyed by the very form of an expression; but language conformations as symbols demonstrably express and influence in fundamental fashion the more persistent interests and values we study and analyze. McLuhan has summarized this facet of communication as follows: "Languages, old and new, as macromyths, have that relation to words and word-making that characterizes the fullest scope of myth. . . . Another way of getting at this aspect of languages as macromyths is to say that the medium is the message. Only incidentally, as it were, is such a medium a specialized means of signifying or of reference. . . . A language is, on the one hand, little affected by the use individuals make of it; but, on the other hand, it almost entirely patterns the character of what is thought, felt, or said by those using it." [4]

In order to identify the meanings of political language styles it is useful to bear in mind a principle often found in symbolic analysis: that there is a formal analogy in logical structure between a symbol and its referent. Langer declares that, "Such formal analogy, or congruence of logical structures, is the prime requisite for the relation between a symbol and whatever it is to mean." [5]

Of the possible meanings of a language style inherent in its structure, the researcher identifies its actual meaning for a particular public by observing their response to it. This procedure accords with Mead's behavioral definition of meaning in terms of response.[6]

What formal properties of political language correspond to the observable responses of interested publics? The analysis that follows will suggest that the following stylistic elements are relevant: commands; definitions; statements of

[4] Marshall McLuhan, "Myth and Mass Media," *Daedalus*, 88 (1959), 340.
[5] Langer, *Feeling and Form*, p. 27. Köhler deals with the proposition exhaustively. Cf. Wolfgang Köhler, *Gestalt Psychology* (New York, reprint 1959), especially Chap. 6.
[6] Mead, *op. cit.*, pp. 78–79.

premises, inferences, and conclusions (i.e., reasoning); forms of expression or settings indicating the public or private character of the originating agency (originator); and forms of expression or settings indicating the public or restricted character of the audience to which the language is addressed (audience).

In various combinations these elements produce four distinctive styles which pervade the governmental process. I identify them as hortatory, legal, administrative, and bargaining language styles. Although the formal properties were identified by the kind of observation to be described below, it is reassuring that they turn out to deal with the relationships of people to government that are regarded, and taught, as basic in our culture. They manifestly deal with authority, persuasion, and participation: with whether people see themselves as ultimately ruler or ruled, included or excluded. Here is initial evidence that the meanings of the styles of political language are the persistent political meanings. It will appear that the meanings of each language style for unorganized, uninvolved mass audiences, as revealed in their responses, are often directly contradictory to its meanings for directly involved groups, as revealed in their behavior. This phenomenon illuminates a central problem of political science: the precise dynamics by which political stability and popular consensus are maintained concurrently with wide freedom of policy maneuver for elites.

What follows is an essay at finding the various meanings of political language forms: the impressions those who use the language convey regardless of the ideas they intend to express. Because the universe of behavioral responses from which to select is vast, the conclusions reached here must be regarded as tentative, and other observers may well differ in emphasis. Responses fall into a rather small number of patterns, however; and the most important conclusions are those about which we can be most confident: that style does convey meaning and that the meaning is a central explanation of political stability or polarization.

We also find reason to suspect that the use of particular language styles is a more sensitive and useful index of political functions in the modern state than the conventional division into executive, legislative, and judicial actions.

II

Hortatory language is especially conspicuous in appeals to particular audiences for policy support, in election campaigns, in legislative debates and hearings, in judicial and administrative *obiter dicta*, and in primary group discussion in all phases of the governmental process. In all these settings people try constantly to persuade others that the policies they espouse should be accepted generally. More directly and clearly than any other, this language style is directed at the mass public.

It is worth noting first that the stable meanings of form associated with this language style are all the more significant because the denotations of its content are so notoriously unstable and ambiguous. Popular semantic analysis concentrates on the terms commonly employed in hortatory language, such as "democracy," "communism," "justice," and the "public interest," and nothing is easier than to show that people read different meanings into them.[7] But a style employed so fervently, formally and informally, by everyone involved in political processes must have social and political functions other than the dissemination of semantic confusion.

The hortatory style consists formally of premises, inferences, and conclusions, some stated and others implied. The conclusions, being promises or threats, amount to appeals for public support, and this generality of appeal is the style's most conspicuous formal element.

Whether or not people agree with a particular appeal, and

[7] Cf. Stuart Chase, *The Tyranny of Words* (New York, 1938). It is demonstrable that not only these obvious cases, but phrases commonly used in this language style which first appear to be more objective are also ambiguous. See p. 137.

in spite of the almost total ambiguity of the terms employed, each instance of the use of this language style in our culture is accepted as evidence of the need for widespread support of public policy. Those to whom appeals are made must be influential. The premises or the reasoning may be disputed, but the assumption that the appeal is necessary and that the public response will in fact influence policy is taken for granted and is strengthened by every serious response. Both denial and support of the soundness of a particular argument bolster the assumption equally effectively. In their every response the affected publics declare their confidence that valid logic and adequate data will guide political agencies to reflect their values or other widespread values.

Popular discussion and criticism of all instances of the use of hortatory language therefore leave little room for doubt about the central meanings of the style itself. The key meanings are popular participation and rationality. Regardless of the specific issue discussed, the employment of this language style is accepted as evidence that the public has an important stake and role in political decisions and that reason and the citing of relevant information is the road to discovering the nature of the stake.

The significance of this response is highlighted if we recall that in some other cultures, both primitive and contemporary, a different myth underlies political processes: that emotion, racial instincts, or blind obedience to charismatic leaders is the road to discovering the nature of the public's stake in governmental policy.[8] In a culture in which science and logic are hallowed as the road to truth, it is to be expected that the state, perhaps our most potent and universal symbol, should emphasize the appeal to reason both in its parliamentary procedures and in formal judicial justifications of decisions. Both in legislative debates and *obiter dicta* there is a formal appeal for support of the policy adopted on the ground that it is logically demonstrable that it will serve the widest public, directly or indirectly.

[8] Cf. Cassirer, *The Myth of the State*, Chaps. 3, 4, 18.

One recent study that is unusually explicit on this point dealt with the formulation of policy in the Illinois legislature. Steiner and Gove found that legislators typically decide how they will vote on bills even before committee hearings are held, as the result of logrolling or understandings about the positions of interested groups. It is nonetheless extremely important that the sponsor of a controversial bill provide a rationalization for those of his supporters who might later be questioned about the reason for their vote. The study explains the device and its differential meanings for legislators and for interested groups very clearly by referring to the testimony of a University of Illinois professor of law, who appeared before a standing committee of the legislature in opposition to a tax bill. Neither the professor nor the legislator who had arranged for his appearance assumed his arguments had swayed any votes.

However [the legislator pointed out], do not undersell the significance of the presentation. Our arrangements [for votes] were concluded before the hearing ever started, but it was absolutely essential that members who had agreed to vote against the bill be furnished with a "cover" — with an impressive witness whose competence was unquestioned so that they could offer an explanation of their votes. The professor furnished that "cover." When we return the favor on legislation in which others are interested, we shall expect to be furnished with a "cover." The more consistently a legislator can furnish a good "cover" to support his position, the easier it is for him to enter into logrolling arrangements.[9]

The crucial character of the potential reaction of interested publics, and the influence of dramatic and rhetorical form upon this reaction, is central to the understanding of this and similar incidents. It is especially revealing that the legislators assume it to be essential that the form of rational discussion be maintained, even when almost no one, inside or

[9] Gilbert Y. Steiner and Samuel K. Gove, *Legislative Politics in Illinois* (Urbana, Ill., 1960), p. 77.

outside the legislature, is paying attention to the content of the argument.

Other responses to the hortatory style support these conclusions. Emotional fervor often crops up in political exhortation in a rather obvious way; but the respectable (i.e., socially reinforced) response to blatant emotionalism in electoral, legislative, or judicial argument is to deplore it. Audiences value gestures and postures consistent with rationality. Hence the most astute and effective use of this language style conceals emotional appeal under the guise of defining issues. The characteristic ambiguity of the key words employed makes this enterprise possible.

In the field of labor policy, for example, all contending groups and their political representatives justify the particular form of governmental regulation they favor on the ground that it will accomplish one or more of the following goals: minimize the harmful effects of strikes, especially on innocent third parties; curb unfair tactics; promote peaceful negotiations; safeguard the public interest; provide minimal economic and social protections for the worker. While these phrases may seem to be objective definitions of issues and are discussed as if they were, they are nothing more than emotional appeals for public support. They appeal to everyone's sense of fairness while concealing conflicts of interest and of intent behind words like "harmful," "innocent," "unfair," "public interest," and "minimal." [10]

The emotional fervor covert or overt in political argument and in reactions to it conveys a sense of the reality of the battle, the importance of the stakes, the gripping quality of the great drama of state. Through participation in it emotionally, it becomes a medium of self-expression, a rite which helps the individual to reflect in action his own interest in, and relationship to, what Lasswell has called a "symbol of the whole."

[10] Cf. Murray Edelman, "Labor Policy in a Democracy," *Current History*, 36 (September, 1959), 96.

The proceeding is thus a good deal more complicated psychologically than extant models of political process are likely to suggest. If the *content* of hortatory political language draws out different responses from different groups, its *form*, for reasons already suggested, calls out the same responses from the mass audience exposed to it. By reinforcing their confidence in the reality of public participation in policy-making and in the central role of reason, it promotes their acceptance of policy. Even in the face of defeat on a particular issue, the assumption is strengthened that debate and reasoning have appealed to the public and protected it, avoiding or minimizing arbitrary, irrational, or self-serving public policy.

If this analysis of the meanings of the form and content of this political language style in the United States is correct, both form and content reinforce the tendency toward a quiescent response to political acts and events. Both make for social harmony through the very fact of disharmony on transient issues.

It is worth noting that the theme of popular participation conveyed through hortatory language turns out to be largely a misleading theme in the light of empirical research. Sampling survey studies concludes that issues and ideologies play a relatively slight part in determining voting behavior,[11] and students of the legislative and judicial processes conclude that debate and hearings often serve either to provide access for small, organized interests or as a ceremony to dramatize the meanings discussed in the last several pages. They are more likely to rationalize legislative and judicial behavior than to influence it.

III

A second distinctive style pervading most of the governmental processes is legal language, encompassing constitutions, treaties, statutes, contracts, bills, and the legally binding portions

[11] Campbell, Converse, Miller, and Stokes, *op. cit.*, Chap. 10.

of judicial decisions. Hundreds of thousands of legal propositions are solemnly propounded every year, their details dimly
sensed but their existence appreciated by the lay population,
their applicability to particular conflict situations debated
and pontificated by lawyers, judges, and administrators.

The obvious approach to defining the meaning of legal
language is to apply the dictionary meanings of the words,
and the layman naturally assumes that this is how the experts
do define its meaning. That laymen make this comforting
assumption is itself an important fact of politics for reasons
that will shortly be explored. But dictionary meanings are
operationally close to irrelevant so far as the function of the
statute or treaty in the political process is concerned. For laymen either never see such language or find it incomprehen-
sible; and its authoritative interpreters, including political
scientists in this case, know that it is in fact almost completely ambiguous in meaning.

It is precisely its ambiguity that gives lawyers, judges, and
administrators a political and social function, for unambiguous rules would, by definition, call neither for interpretation
nor for argument as to their meaning. Whether a statutory
standard is couched in normative language ("the public
interest"), as a directive to seek a particular objective (maintain high levels of employment, rehabilitate a foreign economy, or combat communism), or even as a cardinal number
(a 25-mile-an-hour speed limit), it means what its administrators do about it. Clearly, administrators and judges do
different and even contradictory things while ostensibly carrying out the same legal directive. Because it is not the legal
language that explains the differences, the language is ambiguous.

Operationally, then, the dictionary level of meaning of
legal language functions in two ways: it gives the mass of
citizens a basis for assuming that there is a mechanical, precise, objective definition of law, and it provides a vocabulary
in which organized groups justify their actions to accord with
this lay assumption.

Because the denotations of legal terms are not meaningful to the mass of the population, it is clear that here, as in the case of hortatory language, whatever meanings are conveyed to laymen must be a function of language form and of the setting from which the language issues.

In syntactical form legal language consists almost entirely of definitions and of commands. That these formal elements produce a strong response among the general public is evidenced by the sort of humor regarding legal language that strikes a popular chord, and by the character of the teachings and myths concerning the law that abound in the public schools and in widely read magazines and books. While imprecise, this type of evidence probes exactly the response desired. I hope the conclusions suggested here accord well enough with the reader's own experiences that he is willing to accept them as tentative postulates.

The analogue to legal definitions in popular response is an impression of great precision. When a comedian wants to parody legal language, he strings together a sequence of synonyms, and legal draftsmen do not deviate very far from the parody.

Related to this impression is that of the assurance of popular and legislative supremacy. A language form issuing from popularly elected organs and combining seemingly precise definitions with commands to administrators and judges provides the formal basis for the symbol. The popular response is easily seen in the picture of the process of American government portrayed in high school civics courses, patriotic oratory, and the press, especially when these media are contrasting American with alien systems of government. In this picture there is a continuous, mechanical line of influence from "people" to administration. Statutes reflect the public will, and, being unambiguous and imperative, even as to borderline and improbable future cases, they are "carried out" by courts and administrative agencies. It is less significant that this myth is so commonly presented than that it finds so ready and strong a response, as any American government professor who has tried to question parts of it in class can testify. The practice of denouncing unpopular administrative and judicial actions on the ground that they deviated from the popular and legislative "will" and constituted "judicial legislation" is further evidence for this proposition.

What meaning, on the other hand, does legal language have for those directly involved in interpreting it, as reflected in the uses they make of the language and their actual behavior in carrying out the statutory or treaty rules? The first and most conspicuous characteristic likely to strike the careful observer is flexibility: differing interpretations of the same language with different authorities, changing times, altered conditions, and varying group interests. Nor is there any generally applied or recognized objective test for settling the differences. The ambiguity is neither incidental nor accidental. For lawyers and their organized clients, it is the most useful attribute of legal language. To those directly involved, the meaning of law constantly and observably changes with variations in group influence.[12] To laymen, such influence is an occasional and deplorable deviation from a mythical norm.

It is of some importance to be clear as to exactly what is involved here. Faced with a specific case, administrators and judges proceed as if the language is ambiguous, arguing for the application that will protect their clients or their values and expecting others to argue for alternative interpretations and applications. Questioning a worker about his union membership may not be an "unfair labor practice" today and become one tomorrow, even though Congress has not changed the language of the Taft-Hartley Act at all.[13] The Federal Power Commission may, by judicial fiat, gain new authority to regulate gas rates at the well head.[14] But when faced with an abstract discussion of law, the same judges or

[12] Truman, *op. cit.*, Chaps. 13–15.
[13] Standard-Coosa-Thatcher Co., 85 NLRB 1358 (1949).
[14] *Phillips Petroleum Co. v. Wisconsin*, 347 U.S. 672 (1954).

administrators are likely to talk quite sincerely as if statutory language does have a clear meaning; and elaborate rationalizations for this proposition are spun out and promulgated in *obiter dicta* and news releases.

This is a far more subtle and significant phenomenon than deception. If simple hypocrisy were involved, the whole legal system would soon collapse and be replaced by another more appropriate for expressing and resolving the dilemmas and conflicts of all the elite and lay groups involved. Seen from different perspectives, the variant elite behavior noted here is at once the symbolic satisfaction of reference groups, conflict resolution, and self-expression. For it satisfies both pressure groups and the mass audience and it goes on indefinitely in constantly renewed forms. The elites are products of the same society as the laymen. In their ambivalence they are simply acting for different audiences and reference groups: taking the role of different "others." [15] Both meanings can be strongly held. Their logical incompatibility is quite consonant with their psychological compatibility. A language form which facilitates this result is functional. It is compatible with social and political harmony because laymen and involved elites both share the other's response in precisely those situations in which conflict would otherwise occur.

IV

The style of administrative rules, regulations, and memoranda resembles that of statutes in some respects; but in two major formal elements (originator and audience) and in mass response the styles differ markedly. Here, as in statutes, the imperative mood and precise definitions are conspicuous. Rather than coming from a popularly elected body, however, this kind of language typically originates with appointed officials. The administrator is the only genus of government

[15] Strauss (ed.), *The Social Psychology of George Herbert Mead*, pp. 219–221.

official whose characteristic style of expression does not constantly assert that he exists to carry out the public will. Elected officials do this both in their hortatory language and in their posture of being constantly subject to recall by popular demand. Administrative language, moreover, is addressed to a public or to employees who are expected to comply with its instructions directly and usually immediately. Here is not the legislator, chief executive, or judge whose noble rhetoric and legal acts one reads about in the newspaper, but rather the policeman, postal official, Food and Drug Administrator, or factory inspector with all too real power to help or hurt on the spot or very soon. Inevitably, the intense awareness of his authority and his potential arbitrariness is read into his formal statements.

The public response appears constantly in the two emotional modes of anger and humor: ridicule of administrative jargon and denunciation of administrative pronouncements for their allegedly arbitrary character.

The meaning of the administrative language style is thus closely analogous to the formal elements of the style. It evidently means authority and a closed group acting with arbitrary finality. These meanings are made clear and frequently denounced in popular discussion, TV humor, and political debate. In this sense military regulations are only the polar case of administrative language generally, and the enlisted man's reaction the prototype of a general reaction. That wisecracks and polemics against administrative jargon find a ready market is significant even when it is not justified, for the style evidently suggests a closed elite communicating in a language impenetrable to outsiders. The impenetrability that is taken for granted in statutory language is resented here, and the formal differences in originator and audience explain the difference in response.

It is natural that those who oppose the content of administrative policies should find it so easy to take advantage of this popular response to the administrators' symbolic posture. Thus, businessmen who dislike a public program lead the chorus of ridicule of its administrators; but they find this gambit effective, apparently indefinitely, only because it does demonstrably strike a popular chord even among those who objectively benefit from the administrative program in question, as in the case of OPA. It is also common for legislators to join in this kind of attack on administration, presumably in part because of their realization of their own lesser influence on tangible resource allocations and in part because they have something to gain from demonstrating that they share in the popular response to the administrative style.

While these meanings are clear enough in popular behavior and in the most conspicuous public reactions, there is more ambivalence about the administrative style than is true of the public response to the other styles considered here. When attention is focused upon the governmental process generally, the characteristic response is to the administrator's role in the "mechanical popular sovereignty myth" discussed earlier. To this extent the setting of administrative activity sometimes suggests simply the "carrying out" of popular and legislative policy. But when attention is on a particular directive, the negative responses are more prominent. Responses to the *content* of administrative language naturally complicate things still further, though these are not the main concern of this chapter and involve more transitory political phenomena. While elites are more ambivalent about statutory language, the lay public is apparently more ambivalent about the administrative style.

That the popular conceptions of the administrative process conveyed by administrative language do not jibe with the use of the language form by groups directly involved in the process is made clear by a large body of work in organization theory and in case studies of administrative decision-making. It is an elementary tenet of organization theory that one can formulate an operational definition of authority only by designating as the key element not the arbitrary commands of the nominal superior but rather the willingness of the staff member receiving directives or suggestions to comply with them regardless of his own critical judgment. Compliance creates authority, not the other way around. Influence is exerted from all levels of the organization in response to both internal and external values.[16]

Even more significantly for our purposes, all the general and case studies of administrative policy formation stress the decisive influence on administrative policies of the groups most directly concerned, usually "the regulated." In this sense the administrator, far from being a self-sufficient despot, survives only as long as he responds sensitively enough to the web of groups with access to him and sanctions over him.[17] These groups are often interested in promoting administrative inactivity. There is typically neither authority nor arbitrary finality in the popular sense of these terms. Here is not personal despotism, but resource manipulation in response to group interests.

The significance of the cleavage between mass response and the response of the representatives of organized groups to the style of administrative rules now begins to emerge. The mass response, amounting usually to suspicion and ridicule, encourages administrative timidity and inactivity. The response of the organized often encourages the same thing, though in the former case the response is typically irrational and in the latter case often rational. There are thus built-in tendencies reducing the probability that administrative agencies will deliver the tangible benefits legislatures or executives promise in controversial regulatory statutes or treaties.[18]

V

Because it is used in private, the language of bargaining may not as obviously seem to permeate the political process as the

[16] Simon, *op. cit.*, Chap. 7.

[17] Truman, *op. cit.*, Chap. 14.

[18] For a more detailed analysis of this subject and a statement of some other conditions bearing on the outcome, see Chapter 2.

three styles already discussed. Yet it is an essential catalyst of policy formation in all facets of government.

Like hortatory language, it involves an effort to gain support for a political position; but the two styles are fundamentally different in respect to the occasions of their use, the parties involved, and the meanings conveyed by the respective media. A lobbyist arguing his case in the office of a congressman or administrator normally uses hortatory language: he suggests a rationalization that would justify the public official in granting him what he wants. But the rationalization, if it is persuasive, is so precisely because it would satisfy an interested public. The whole interaction can be understood as an effort to feed some premises about a potential public reaction into a legislative, administrative, or judicial decision-making process.

The bargainer, on the other hand, offers a deal, not an appeal. A public reaction is to be avoided, not sought. A decision is to be made through an exchange of quid pro quos, not through a rational structuring of premises so as to maximize, or satisfice, values. It is a prerequisite to bargaining that values be incompatible, not shared.[19]

Once these conditions are specified, examples of political bargaining are not hard to find. Negotiations in a slating committee regarding the conditions for support of an aspirant for a place on the ticket, logrolling in a legislature, bribery, negotiations among representatives of administrative agencies with clashing policy predilections in the same area are all of this type. The very establishment of an interagency committee normally constitutes recognition of the need for bargaining. From the National Security Council and the Joint Chiefs of Staff on down to the hundreds of unpublicized committees like the Interdepartment Radio Advisory Committee, bargaining catalyzes governmental procedures.

To list examples of political bargaining is to illustrate the fact that some instances of it have an unsavory reputation

19 Robert A. Dahl and Charles E. Lindblom, *Politics, Economics, and Welfare* (New York, 1953), Chaps. 10, 11.

while others are widely approved. That is to say, the meaning of this activity is sometimes the view that the public interest is being carefully safeguarded by knowledgeable sages (as in the case of the National Security Council) and sometimes the view that unscrupulous "interests" are plotting for private gain at the public's expense (as in the cases of logrolling, bribery, secret treaty negotiations, and often slate-making). The basis of the distinction is an assumption about the nature of the interaction. Where instances of bargaining are regarded with approval, it is precisely because it is popularly (if sometimes mistakenly) assumed that groups like the National Security Council and the Joint Chiefs of Staff engage not in bargaining but in rational devising of means of achieving goals to benefit the public generally. To the extent that it is suggested that the participants are engaged in making deals to promote the interests of their own services, agencies, or economic groupings, the proceedings are looked upon with suspicion rather than favor. In these cases not even the setting (i.e., originator and audience) suggests a formal tie to the people and the "legislative will," as in the case of administrative activity. On the contrary, the setting and the language both emphasize private dealing to evade popular sovereignty, and the public response reflects this meaning.

Because bargaining is private by its very nature and the actual language of the negotiations normally never publicized, the significant formal element conveying meaning to the public is the setting: specifically the parties involved in the bargain. The privacy also facilitates public misconceptions about the extent to which the negotiations involve inclusion or exclusion of the interests of those not present. Empirical studies frequently suggest that such misconceptions occur. More often than not, perhaps, they involve an assumption that the bargaining is safeguarding a wide public when the more accurate keynote is exclusion.[20] To the extent

[20] For case studies suggesting this conclusion, see Steiner, *op. cit.*; Murray Edelman, "Governmental Organization and Public Policy," *Public Administration Review*, 12 (Autumn, 1952), 276–283.

that such a bias in meaning occurs systematically, we have another instance of a meaning conveyed by form promoting social harmony and quiescence.

It is therefore hardly surprising that the image participants in such agencies try to disseminate is one which ignores and conceals their bargaining function, emphasizing the alleged purpose of protecting the public generally. The adverse response to use of the bargaining medium might otherwise become so intense as to endanger the continuation of a convenient forum in which to carry on necessary bargaining.

So far as the meaning of bargaining language to the bargainers themselves is concerned, there is very little ambiguity where bargains have actually occurred. It is of the essence that the quid pro quos be clear, and that any ambiguity be deliberate, be recognized as such, and be tolerated only as a means of getting agreement on unambiguous central issues. This aspect of the dealing and of the language is, however, strictly private. The absence of public response is one of its prerequisites, for reasons already suggested.

Where, as in treaty negotiations, there is sometimes intense public pressure upon both parties to announce an agreement, the terms may of course be ambiguous. But ambiguous language here is evidence of the absence of bargaining or of its failure. Such failure is clear to the parties involved in the negotiations, though the public response is not a function of the failure, as the "spirit of Geneva" illustrates. What is involved here is a substitution of hortatory language for bargaining. Such instances of combinations of language forms are discussed later.

The focus of attention in bargaining negotiations is upon the power positions of the two parties, and a certain amount of feinting and feeling out of positions is typically necessary; but the terms of the final agreement are relatively clear where bargaining has occurred. The best possible evidence for this proposition lies in the fact that deviation from such understandings is routinely denounced as deception. This charge is conspicuously not made in the case of deviations from the connotations of other language styles, which occur routinely as reflections of the differential meanings of these languages to various publics and which at worst are condemned as unwise, misinterpretation, or power-seeking.

VI

When these language styles are compared with each other in the order in which they are considered here, a rather significant observation emerges. The disparity between the connotations of each style for the mass public and for direct participants grows smaller as one moves from the hortatory style to the bargaining style — moves, in fact, from settings in which they are almost completely contradictory to those in which there is no disparity. At the same time, the involvement of a wide public grows progressively smaller. Putting the two observations together, we conclude that meanings conveyed to mass publics are consistently different from those reflected in the responses of small, immediately involved groups; but the mass public progressively disappears as a factor as policy definition moves toward the allocation of tangible values. The significant function of the hortatory style is its reassurance of a mass public so that directly involved groups may function more freely in the later policy-making stages. Mass responses to the legal and administrative styles are important conditioning factors, though organized groups interpret both styles so as to serve their own ends, and logically incompatible responses emerge in different situations. In the case of bargaining, avoidance of a mass public response and of clear awareness that bargaining is even taking place is sought. Groups with power and benefits to trade do the negotiating and reach common meanings.

The fact that specific political situations almost always involve the use of more than one language style facilitates political conflict resolution in several ways. It is typically through administration and bargaining that political groups secure tangible rather than symbolic benefits; but these are the styles that arouse public suspicion. The fact that bargaining and administration always occur in close conjunction with hortatory or legal language makes it easy for mass publics to underestimate the importance of the two less popular styles and to overestimate the importance for resource allocations of the hortatory and legal styles, the two that convey symbolic reassurance. In the legislative process it is the floor speeches and the ringing declarations (the "cover"), not the logrolling, that are assumed to be decisive. The Shakespearean and biblical rhetoric that John L. Lewis employed as an obligato to his negotiations with employers was hortatory, identifying him with the symbols of righteousness. Lewis was engaged simultaneously in trying to maximize his support among the miners and the public generally and in driving a bargain with the employers. The assumption that the rhetorical flourishes were the weapons that explained specific contract victories was useful to Lewis as a political figure in the union, but should not confuse a social scientist. It is well known to mediators that hortatory language inside a bargaining session is a signal of failure to agree, not of bargaining.

More than that, the greater the failure, the clearer the denial of benefits to the publics expecting them, the more intense is the barrage of hortatory and legal language likely to be. The occurrence of such a barrage may normally be accepted as evidence of the failure. Sometimes such signals of a breakdown in a quest for tangible benefits or bargaining occurs in the form of hortatory language inserted into the actual text of a statute or treaty. As already noted above, all legal language is ambiguous; but a legal declaration that benefits are to be awarded in accordance with "the public interest," for example, is at once a declaration that the claims of the ostensible beneficiaries have not in fact been granted and a symbolic reassurance that they have.

Recognition of the transactional tie among language, experience, and meaning thus enables us to utilize linguistic analysis to probe a facet of political dynamics that is otherwise difficult to observe. It also offers a sensitive tool for political analysis of a more microscopic kind. With it we can easily isolate the hortatory, legal, administrative, and bargaining activities within each of the traditional categories of electoral, legislative, administrative, and judicial behavior and thereby explore more realistically the meanings of behaviors and expressions.

The analysis of language styles should help clear up some misleading impressions conveyed by our continued reliance on Montesquieu's categories. It reveals which groups are using what tactics and with what effect. It forces continual inquiry about political tactics and symbolizing rather than tempting us into assuming that authoritative declarations of "policy" are predictors of subsequent resource allocations.

A similar analysis of other cultures would no doubt bring to light different typologies of language forms, with different persisting meanings; but for each culture the message conveyed by form would be expected to express either commonly cherished myths or fundamental divisions in the society.

The network of social alliances cemented by these meanings constitutes a framework upon which evanescent political alliances and interests are built and a rhetoric in which they are expressed and related to more enduring interests and myths. In our culture these language styles strongly promote social cohesion. The candidate, legislator, administrator, or lobbyist inevitably, through the very language he employs, expresses both his current interests and the underlying myths that enable him to have his impact and his access.

CHAPTER 8

Persistence and Change
in Political Goals

Political analyses frequently assume that men have political goals or interests which they try to satisfy and that their political discontent is stilled in the measure that these goals are achieved. Attitudinal surveyors apparently make the same assumption, and so do their respondents. Journalists and political science studies commonly take it for granted that particular groups "want" white supremacy or higher pay or job security or the victory of the free world; that such interests will persist and determine political support or opposition until they are realized; and that they will then no longer persist. The assumption is not so much defended as unexamined.

It fits neatly into a rational view of society and into an orientation that emphasizes popular participation as the keynote of politics. There is accordingly a built-in bias in favor of its acceptance in our society. But there is also compelling evidence against its validity. If the common assumption is false, that fact has significant implications for (1) the relationship of future political demands to present ones; (2) the utility of the very concept of political goals or objectives; and (3) the meaning of responses to attitudinal surveys. In any case it is clearly important to understand the social, psychological, and linguistic processes underlying changes in the character and intensity of mass political goals and the modes of expressing them. This chapter tries to further that understanding.

1

Normally, the achievement of a declared political objective not only fails to put to rest the political interest in question, but also leads to the advancement of more ambitious claims of the same general character as the satisfied claim. The evidence for this assertion consists both of readily accessible observations of instances of public policy formation and of pertinent research in related social science disciplines. This chapter reviews this evidence and advances a hypothesis. The theory of persistence and flux in political interests considered here consists of several facets, only some of which are clearly established by the available evidence. Other facets are suggested by what we know, but the evidence for them is not conclusive.

The thesis to be considered can be summarized as follows. Except under conditions which can be largely specified, (1) success in achieving a political objective leads to demands for larger amounts of the same benefits or to new goals different in manifest content but like the old ones in respect to a latent dimension; (2) failure to achieve a political objective leads to its abandonment or to a more modest objective; (3) the terms conventionally cited as naming political objectives, being logical and formal categories rather than empirical descriptions, do not name, predict, or control behavior but do evoke anxieties and hopes; (4) quiescence with respect to political objectives is a function of various forms of symbolic reassurance; (5) certain types of political objections not satisfied symbolically are likely to erupt into direct, extragovernmental mass action; (6) these generalizations hold for the time spans with which political analysis normally deals, but most of them are a function of the persistence of reference groups which may eventually disappear.

Observations that point toward the operational definition of the terms we call political goals are of various kinds. Some general observations are summarized in the present section, preceding a discussion in the next two sections of research findings which help explain them and point up their implications.

1. Goals or interests continue to evoke political discontent regardless of the extent to which the claims they name are fulfilled, except under rigidly defined conditions considered below.

Whether some Southerners successfully prevent Negroes in their county from voting or fail in the attempt, they still respond strongly and favorably to the term "white supremacy." The "victory of the free world" remains a potent evocative symbol regardless of whether the cold war is currently cooler or warmer or whether we have won or lost the last cold war battle. Workers always want "higher pay," whether they are currently making fifty dollars a week or three hundred dollars a week. Advocates of governmental economy continue to support austerity and oppose appropriations after successes in achieving this aim and regardless of the degree of their success.

2. A group whose declared political objective defined in measurable terms is completely satisfied predictably advances a claim for larger quantities of the same benefit.

Consider those cases in which the amount of the public benefit is objectively observable, as in social security benefits, minimum wage guarantees, or free public education. Enactment of legislation and the establishment of agencies to administer such programs ends initial intense agitation for the benefits, but in every case demands for larger quantities or higher qualities of the benefits in question quickly crop up.

Benefits and coverage of the Social Security Act, for example, have been increased by almost every Congress since World War II, with relatively little legislative controversy in most instances. Demands for a higher minimum wage and for wider coverage of the Fair Labor Standards Act are constant, and the Act has been amended to meet them in 1949, 1955, and 1960. We can be confident that the process will continue.

It is untenable in the light of what we know of leadership theory to assume that the new claims are regarded with hostility or apathy by the masses who supported the initial ones. Success in such cases has consistently bred more confident and intensified interest in a larger claim, not satiation.

3. A group whose political objective is achieved advances claims for other types of benefits, where the satisfied claims and the new ones lie upon a common latent value continuum.

This more complicated expression of the same psychopolitical phenomenon must be regarded with more tentativeness; but a great deal of empirical and theoretical evidence points to its validity, and its implications for policy formation are far-reaching. The suggestion is that success in achieving certain types of political goals will predictably lead to claims upon related goals. Research has already demonstrated that in many policy areas there is a common latent attribute underlying a number of values with differing content. This is the contribution of the many studies that have found that particular political values form a Guttman scale. Guttman has declared that the "crucial thing" in such research is discovering "evidence of the degree to which the manifest items satisfy criteria of unidimensionality";[1] and Lazarsfeld has written of "the basic idea of latent structure analysis, namely, that all the association between any two items is due to the latent attribute, and that there is no association between the specific components of the items."[2]

If a common dimension underlies sets of political goals differing in manifest content, and if achievement of an aspiration level leads to a higher aspiration level,[3] we would expect

[1] Samuel A. Stouffer and others, *The American Soldier: Studies in Social Psychology in World War II*, Vol. 4 (Princeton, 1950), pp. 25–26.

[2] *Ibid.*, p. 29.

[3] This assumption about aspiration levels has long been borne out by experimental research. The question is considered below.

that satisfaction of a political goal would be succeeded by the advancement of another goal with different manifest content but lying upon the same underlying dimension.

Many sets of political values satisfactorily meeting the necessary criteria for a Guttman scale have now been identified, and it may therefore be assumed that a latent common dimension exists. The Survey Research Center, for example, analyzing political attitudes of 1956, has identified sets of opinions in both the domestic and foreign policy areas which form satisfactory Guttman scales. A "social welfare" value structure includes items on aid to education, medical care, employment guarantees, FEPC and Negro housing, and public versus private production of electricity and housing. Such other domestic issues as the role of big business in government, tax levels, and governmental social welfare activity were found empirically to be excluded from the scale, thereby defining the boundaries of this particular value structure.[4]

It is, moreover, one of the most common political phenomena that the satisfaction of claims in some policy area generates claims in related areas, and where a succession of such claims are gratified, we see sudden bursts of governmental action in fields previously left to private activity. The proliferation of state labor legislation in 1910–11,[5] the New Freedom, the New Deal, and the Fair Deal all represent such patterns, and many other examples could be cited from the history of the United States and other countries. We also know that it is largely the same individuals who support the successive objectives in such value structures and the same individuals who oppose them.

It must be said, however, that these evidences fall considerably short of establishing the hypothesis. A major difficulty in building more definitive proof lies in the fact that the various items hypothesized to lie upon a common underlying dimension would have to be postulated in advance and

[4] Campbell, Converse, Miller, and Stokes, *op. cit.*, pp. 194–195.
[5] Elizabeth Brandeis, "Labor Legislation," in John R. Commons and associates, *History of Labor in the United States*, Vol. 3 (New York, 1935).

the flow of events then used to test the validity of the hypothesis. Retrospective evidence of the type cited here cannot be conclusive. The hypothesis suggested here nonetheless offers promise of explaining the precise dynamics of a political phenomenon we have too long been content to designate as an occasional flareup of reform sentiment or in some such vague way.

4. Unambiguous failure of a group to achieve a political objective is followed by a lowering of the aspiration level.

One can easily cite a long list of political goals once pressed and now moderated or changed to more modest alternatives: nationalization of railroads, recall of judges, free trade, incorporation of labor unions, and so on. We hear now of regulation of railroads in the passengers', shippers', or workers' interest, reform in judicial selection, trade agreements, specific alternative regulations of unions, and so on. Such moderation of objectives is precisely the contrary of what the common assumption would suggest: that failure should increase efforts to attain political goals.

II

These observations suggest that satisfaction of political claims generates further claims lying upon a common dimension and that unambiguous obstacles to their satisfaction may moderate or end specific claims. There is an impressive body of linguistic and psychological theory which support the observations just noted.

Some findings about the social and psychological functions of language, to be found in the work of cultural anthropologists and students of linguistic theory, are fundamental. The line of analysis their studies suggest has not often been applied to political language, but it suggests some exciting possibilities.

What exactly is a political goal? It is a name, a label suggested by our dominant cultural values and conceptions: "white supremacy," "higher wages," "urban renewal," "preservation of the free world." It is presented to our attention and calls for a response. But every name is a metaphor.[6] It specifies some property which a class of objects has in common. It thereby calls attention to that property and by the same token draws attention away from other properties. The name "table" calls attention to a flat, raised surface suitable for eating or writing but ignores other properties of the wood and spaces comprising a table. The term "white supremacy" calls attention to differences in skin color, associated differences in power and status relationships, and all the myths these concepts evoke. It is in a different universe of discourse from the flesh and blood white and Negro people working and mingling in specific places in all their multifaceted concreteness. In the actual situation the stimuli include all the facts and values impinging on the participant. Behavior will then be a function of many cross-pressures, some making for cooperation and some for hostility. But when a nonparticipant is called upon to respond to the name abstracted from the situation, he is likely to respond to the supremacy-subordination dimension, for this is what the name "white supremacy" highlights. Like the names of all controversial political goals this metaphor evokes a dimension around which reference groups will have built strong expectations, thereby further reinforcing the hold this dimension has upon the nonparticipating respondent. Some further implications of reference group theory for political goals appear below.

Implicit in this illustration is the assumption that the responses metaphorical terms evoke are not constant. They are a function not only of the language itself, but of the interests, hopes, and fears endemic in the culture or subculture. "White supremacy" as the name of a political objective evokes different responses in northern liberals and in southern racists, as "higher pay" does in workers and managers.

The terms conventionally used to name political goals are therefore logical and formal in character, not empirical. They

[6] Cassirer, *An Essay on Man*, pp. 142, 173; Langer, *Philosophy in a New Key*, pp. 114–115.

are a priori categories we employ to classify perceptions of the political world. They do not originate with observations of behavior, and they clearly do not and cannot predict or control any behavior except the verbal associations already implicit in the formal categories.

This argument that names do not control behavior is worth making only because it is a prevalent myth that they do. Mass satisfaction with our political system depends in part upon widespread acceptance of the myth; and much political analysis is confused by its implicit acceptance as well. We know from administrative behavior studies that the decisions actually granting tangible benefits are a function of a wide range of factual and value premises, as brought into some kind of perspective in an organization. Yet the widespread assumption — further spread by all the popularized references to the American governmental process — is that public response to value choices is the key determinant of policy, that is, that the names of these goals predict and control future behavior.

The myth is a stabilizing social influence, and its persistence is favored by an atavistic response to language upon which anthropologists have placed a great deal of emphasis. In their study of meaning Ogden and Richards observe: "From the earliest times the Symbols which men have used to aid the process of thinking and to record their achievements have been a continuous source of wonder and illusion. The whole human race has been so impressed by the properties of words as instruments for the control of objects, that in every age it has attributed to them occult powers."[7] Edward Sapir documents a related but broader point: "Language is heuristic . . . (in the) sense that its forms predetermine for us certain modes of observation and interpretation. This means of course that as our scientific experience

[7] Ogden and Richards, *op. cit.*, p. 24. See also Malinowski, "The Problem of Meaning in Primitive Languages," in Ogden and Richards, *ibid.*, pp. 322–323, where the same point is illustrated with examples from primitive peoples' behavior.

grows we must learn to fight the implications of language." [8]

To recognize that the names of political goals are formal categories is to recognize that they connote logical possibilities. And if they are politically controversial, the possibilities they evoke have strong emotional effect. That is to say, they name ideals or threats, or, more accurately, a combination of the two, with either the ideal or the threat a possibility, depending upon the course of governmental action. For specifiable groupings each term names both a source of anxiety (black supremacy, starvation pay, unemployment, etc.) and a promise of salvation. It is a symbol, predictably evoking a response looking toward the desirable polar situation. What is desirable for one social cross-section may, however, be the undesirable pole for another. White supremacy may be seen instead as exploitation, starvation pay as low labor costs, and so on. The same dimensions are involved, but they evoke opposite responses, depending on the reference group to which the respondent looks.

It is an interesting commentary on this function of the names of political goals that both psychoanalytic theory and linguistic theory make much of man's tendency to employ the same symbol to connote opposites:[9] that is, to name a category of perceptions grouped between two poles which powerfully focuses attention, anxieties, and hopes. It is not to be expected that the focussing or the direction of the response to logical possibilities should be affected by public or private action to change the quantity of tangible benefits people get. Possibilities remain regardless of actualities.

This kind of analysis does not offer a full explanation of persistence or flux in political interests, but it is a major facet of the political transaction, providing a channel and a tendency for the uninvolved mass public.

It also has obvious implications for the understanding of the transaction that occurs when an interviewer studying atti-

[8] Sapir, *Culture, Language and Personality*, p. 7.
[9] Sigmund Freud, "The Antithetical Meaning of Primal Words," in *Essays on Creativity and the Unconscious* (New York, 1958), pp. 55–62.

tudes confronts a respondent. Louis Guttman has made the undeniable point that, "If we look at the research carried out on attitudes in the past . . . we find it is based largely on verbal behavior." [10]

We can now summarize and point up some implications of these comments for mass behavior and for the study of mass behavior. The formal categories that name political goals are to be understood as *expressions* of culturally created values, not as causes of them. They accordingly tell us about prevailing values in the subcultures we observe. The fact that these names evoke visions of utopia or fears of destruction in large numbers of people accounts for their persistence as potent political symbols. They become the categories within which political thinking and the justification or denunciation of policies must be phrased; and in this sense they may fairly be termed "socially pathic" language,[11] serving as catalysts, though not as generators, of mass behavior that is often irrational.

All of this helps explain persistence and change in political interests, the intensity of interests, and the meaning of political acts and events. It cannot by itself explain public policy formation, for interests find expression in policy only in the degree that they serve as premises for decisions in organizations. Chapters 3 and 4, which deal with some symbolic aspects of organization and leadership, try to place these propositions in conjunction with pertinent organization and leadership theory.

III

If political goals are logical categories evoking a persisting response, the political process may be viewed as a succession of trials to achieve increasingly difficult and gratifying objec-

[10] Stouffer and others, *op. cit.*, p. 48.

[11] The term is suggested by Charles Morris. For a discussion of socially pathic language in general, see Chapter 6.

tives or more modest objectives, along a unidimensional scale. Aspiration level research is therefore also relevant to the understanding of changes in the level of political objectives. The findings that have emerged from many years of such research are also in line with the conclusions reached here and are quite incompatible with the assumption that goals are abandoned when they are achieved.

Indeed, the key finding of aspiration level experiments suggests precisely the opposite: "Habitual success increases aspiration level and habitual failure decreases it." [12] Recent success or failure has an especially strong effect. [13] We have already noted that groups with political aspirations behave in this way.

The psychological experiments have also demonstrated that valence (wishes and fears) has a significant bearing upon aspiration level. [14] Where the affect attaching to a political goal is high, this research would lead us to expect an exaggeration in the impact of success or failure upon aspiration level. I am not aware of any political observations that might either confirm or question this hypothesis.

The research on aspiration levels provides preliminary support for the hypothesis proposed above regarding the emergence of aspirations for new political goals lying upon a common latent dimension with goals already achieved. When the findings of that research are placed in conjunction with Guttman scale research findings about latent value dimensions, we may have some confidence that particular values lying along such a dimension will be sought successively as lower scale values are achieved. Especially pertinent to this suggestion is the conclusion that, "The transfer effect of suc-

[12] Kurt Lewin, Tamara Dembo, Leon Festinger, and Pauline S. Sears, "Level of Aspiration," in J. McVicker Hunt, *Personality and the Behavior Disorders*, Vol. I (New York, 1944), p. 341. My colleague Denis Sullivan has been most helpful in clarifying the relevance of aspiration level research.

[13] *Ibid.*, pp. 367, 373.

[14] *Ibid.*, p. 372.

cess and failure is greatest when the subject finds the two tasks to be similar or two parts of one larger activity." [15]

In one major respect we find a political analogue for some findings of the experiments on aspiration levels. The experimenters made the following findings: "In fields of activity . . . where (a person) is unable to judge his probable performance, the individual frequently does not spontaneously set himself a definite level of aspiration. Instead he goes into the action without definite goal level. . . ." [16]

We have noticed already that for some political demands the exact amount of the public benefit is objectively observable, as in the case of claims for social security benefits and minimum wage protection. In such instances initial successes are succeeded by new claims upon specific larger quantities of the benefits in question.

For certain other types of political claims, it is impossible to observe or reach general agreement on the amount of the benefits granted or even on whether there have been any benefits. This has been the pattern with respect to such issues as antitrust policy and utility rate controls. In such cases legislative standards have been notably vague, and administration has been vacillating, arbitrary, and, in the view of the most careful scholars, pointless or ineffective. This dubious level of accomplishment has nonetheless been tolerated for many decades, with only scattered and politically insignificant demands for higher levels of achievement. The picture fits nicely the more general experimental conclusions quoted above. Probable or even actual performance cannot be judged, and there is in consequence no definite goal level.

IV

What, then, can be said about the conditions of intensity and quiescence in political interests? Here again, we get some

15 *Ibid.*, p. 349.
16 *Ibid.*, p. 366.

help from research findings in related fields, but must then go on to new hypotheses based upon more strictly political observations.

Many years ago Harold Lasswell explained political interest as "the displacement of private affects upon public objects."[17] In this formulation intensity of the political interests could presumably be assumed to be a function of the intensity of the private affects. More recently, Smith, Bruner, and White, with the advantage of three additional decades of research and thought, have suggested that opinions serve three functions for the personality:[18] object appraisal, social adjustment, and externalization. Others have come to impressively similar conclusions.

Politics may now be viewed, again in Lasswell's terms, as "the process by which the irrational bases of society are brought out into the open. . . . It begins in conflict and eventuates in a solution. But the solution is not the 'rationally best' solution, but the emotionally satisfactory one." [19]

Politics, then, can usefully be regarded, in one of its aspects at least, as a powerful congeries of rite and myth through which object appraisal, social adjustment, and externalization are realized. We can, however, be considerably more specific about the conditions of its effectiveness in this respect.

A general hypothesis may be formulated as follows: The intensity of an interest in a particular political objective is lessened in the degree that there is (1) constitutional, statutory, or administrative action dedicating "the state" to achieving the objective, and (2) frequently renewed ritualistic assertion, overt or implicit, that the objective is being achieved. Both the types of public programs discussed above — those offering occasional incremental increases in benefits and those relying upon regular but vague assertions that a threat is being checked — meet these two conditions. Programs of both types demonstrably maintain quiescence, apparently indefi-

17 Lasswell, *Psychopathology and Politics.*
18 Smith, Bruner, and White, *op. cit.*
19 Lasswell, *Psychopathology and Politics*, p. 184.

nitely. It is thus only some form of symbolic reassurance that can be expected to satisfy a symbolic goal.

V

An important qualification must be entered. Many examples have been cited of the failure of tangible benefits to satisfy or end political claims, and the probability of such failure has been suggested through a consideration of the symbolic meaning of the language forms in which political claims are conventionally stated and through attention to aspiration level and scaling research. It is true, however, that certain specific claims do pass from the political scene when they are granted, and the relevance of such phenomena needs to be explored. Slavery, the lame-duck Congressional session, and the denial of the suffrage because of sex were all highly controversial political issues in America at various periods of our history, and all of them passed from view when their opponents' claims were granted (in all of these instances by formal constitutional amendment). Despite these and other tangible benefits to the claimants, however, these latter groups remain active and demanding in the same policy areas. The Negro's claim to specific social, economic, and political benefits and demands for an equitable voice for constituents in Congress and for specific controls over elective officials continue as major themes in American politics. They must do so, for in this more general form they constitute formal categories which represent important values in our culture and are, therefore, inherently insatiable so long as they perform the functions of object appraisal, social adjustment, and externalization. The specific benefits granted by the thirteenth, nineteenth, and twentieth Constitutional amendments are logically equivalent to the granting of a seventy-five cent minimum wage under the Fair Labor Standards Act in 1949. That statute ended the seventy-five cent demand as a political claim, but the higher minimum wage remains a very potent political issue. To the social scientist the continuity of political claims upon the values ranking high in our culture, regardless of specific grants of benefits, must be the important principle and one that has major implications for all analyses of public policy formation.

The reference groups supporting particular values may disappear, or new ones may appear over long periods of time, explaining long-run changes in high-ranking values. People respond to key terms in the way they think specific other groups expect them to respond. The worker, spending much of his life in a factory working with other employees, is likely to choose these other employees as his "significant others." [20] In their role as employees (rather than as Catholics, Poles, whites, or high school graduates) he expects them to respond favorably to the symbol "higher wages," and he does so himself, thereby reinforcing their expectations and being reinforced in his own. A white southerner is likely to choose as his reference group other white southerners; and in their role as white southerners (rather than workers, church members, etc.) he expects them, and cues them to expect him, to respond favorably to the symbol "white supremacy." Where there is no factory economy, or where there is not a substantial Negro population, these roles and symbols do not emerge as significant and persisting features of the environment. A factory economy and a large Negro population being persisting features of our environment, the roles and symbols associated with each of them also persist for long historical periods.

For the time periods with which almost all rigorous political analysis is concerned, reference groups with respect to high-ranking values may be regarded as constants, and the propositions suggested here accordingly remain pertinent.

[20] For fundamental theoretical and empirical work on role theory see Mead, *op. cit.*; N. Gross, W. S. Mason, and A. W. McEachern, *Explorations in Role Analysis* (New York, 1958); E. C. Tolman, "A Psychological Model," in Talcott Parsons and Edward A. Shils, *Toward a General Theory of Action* (Cambridge, 1952); Theodore M. Newcomb, *Personality and Social Change* (New York, 1943).

VI

We can now consider more systematically under what conditions direct extragovernmental mass action to claim resources or suppress counterclaims occurs. When is quiescence lacking? The forms such mass action takes are: revolutions, political strikes and demonstrations, farmers' demonstrations and violence, and vigilante movements. The general principle, as already suggested, is that restiveness occurs when the state is not symbolically aligned with those who feel threatened. Social psychology and organizational theory help explain the particular forms that instances of restiveness take.

For vigilante movements and "radical right" movements both psychological and socioeconomic explanations have been offered. The individuals attracted to such activities have been shown to suffer from "anomie," Durkheim's term for alienation from warm and meaningful social relationships, which is another way of characterizing the absence of symbolic reassurance. Such people, feeling intensely alone, are likely to assume that the threats they perceive are caused by a conspiracy of hostile elements. Their behavior takes on the characteristics that have come to be called "mass society": extreme susceptibility to suggestions for mob action, intolerance, easy excitability, ready arousal to violence. The vigilante action such groups initiate is irrational in the sense that there is no logical reason it should allay the threat they fear or produce the benefits they claim. It is often not clear whether a threat objectively exists. The succession of nativist movements in American history, the antiradical hysteria after World War I, and the McCarthyism of 1951 to 1954 exemplify this kind of departure from political quiescence.

Notice that the vigilante type of mass action is fundamentally pessimistic. Viewing the situation from the perspective of the vigilantes themselves, even a victory would not produce a better world; at best it will remove a potential foe or threat. Victory, moreover, never occurs. The threat that is feared is not based upon observable conditions; and the goal, like all political goals, is a normative category and not a specific empirical state of affairs. Tangible action or benefits therefore cannot bring satisfaction. On the contrary, everything that happens is perceived by the vigilantes as further confirmation of their initial assumptions and of the continued and growing reality of the threat. Symbolic reassurance, periodically renewed and legitimized, may eventually produce quiescence; or changed conditions may bring new personal satisfactions to many of the movement's adherents, reducing their need to discover and attack conspiracies.

There is some evidence that vigilantism is especially likely to occur in periods of economic prosperity.[21] Nativist, antiradical, white supremacy, and other movements of the vigilante types have appeared conspicuously in the prosperous twenties, the fifties, and at high points of the business cycle earlier in American history; but the mass movements and violence of the depressed decade of the thirties took other forms. Vigilante movements have included the most prosperous and the least prosperous. Economic class differences are forgotten in an emotional concern with an enemy difficult to identify who pervades society and who threatens the social order adherents would like to restore or dream about. There may be 205 of him in the State Department and thousands of him in other key places, and the fact that he evaporates when you try to pin him down only proves his elusiveness and cleverness and the prevalence of assisting dupes. The alienation from one's neighbor is consistent with the anomie theory. The fears of the prosperous, the established, and those who identify with a real or imagined Establishment for the continuance of a social order in which their norms are legitimate underlines the pessimistic outlook of these movements.

The other forms direct mass action takes are essentially alike in respect to the symbolic elements of concern here, and they differ in this fundamental respect from vigilantism.

[21] S. M. Lipset, "The Sources of the Radical Right," in Daniel Bell (ed.), *The New American Right* (New York, 1955), pp. 166–234; Richard Hofstadter, "The Pseudo-Conservative Revolt," in Bell, *ibid.*, pp. 33–55.

Participants in revolution, political strikes, and farmers' violence are basically optimistic: they seek and expect a world wholly or partly remade closer to the heart's desire. What animates adherents of these movements is not a desperate fear that a good order will be destroyed, as in the case of vigilantes, but rather a hope that a bad order will be changed or overthrown so that they can come into their own. The badness is seen as neither inevitable nor likely to be changed by any social or governmental device already operating. That is to say, the state is not offering adequate symbolic reassurance. On the contrary, its values are the wrong ones. Rather than the middle class, it perpetuates a feudal nobility in power. Rather than the proletariat, it perpetuates a decadent bourgeoisie in power. Rather than guaranteeing the workers a decent living standard, its laws are rigged to further enrich the employer. Rather than compensating the farmer as the basic producer deserves, it exploits him in behalf of city people. These are the symbolic terms in which revolutions, political strikes, and farmer demonstrations are justified, and they all embody an ameliorative aim.

There is an implicit premise here. Supporters of rebellion, political strikes, and farmers' demonstrations compare their current living standards with better ones and see reason to believe they can achieve the better ones. Their grievances are not predestined or inevitable.

This premise comports well with the findings of historians of revolution.[22] Men are not willing to revolt when they are destitute or the ground-down heirs of centuries of servitude and hopelessness, but rather after they have experienced sufficient improvement in their living standards that it becomes reasonable to assume that improvement is normal and to be expected. They then begin to take as their reference groups not their peers but those better off than they. This promotes restiveness and revolt if there has not been assurance that normal governmental procedures will elevate them to the

[22] Brinton, *op. cit.*; Lyford P. Edwards, *The Natural History of Revolution* (Chicago, 1927).

status of these new reference groups. Here, too, the quantity of tangible benefits offered and their absolute level are thus incapable of producing political quiescence. What is controlling is the significant symbol created by taking the role of a more fortunate reference group.

A number of sociologists have suggested that there is a basic distinction between interest politics, involving groups striving for economic benefits, and status politics, involving groups striving to maintain or improve their status in the social order.[23] Adherents of vigilante or radical right movements as well as temperance groups are cited as examples of groups seeking status through politics. The argument of this chapter suggests that the distinction between interest politics and status politics is not fundamental. If successive grants of higher economic benefits help define a group and give it status, both interest and status are always involved. Similarly, fundamentalist Protestants, temperance groups, and McCarthyites have immediate concrete demands that are instances of a general claim to status. Status and interest are thus aspects of each other and not empirically distinct.

So far as extragovernmental mass action or extremist politics are concerned, there is a key distinction in strategy, and the dichotomy might better be based upon that factor. Strikes by workers or farmers and rebellion are optimistic in outlook and are based upon a concerted plan for a changed order. Vigilante action is pessimistic in outlook, with no plan for a social order perceived as different or better, but with a continuing need on the part of individuals to discover or create, and then harass, groups perceived as threats.

. . . .

Our political institutions constitute, among other things, a device for providing symbolic reassurance to threatened groups, and the device works admirably for most issues. In the United States instances of direct extragovernmental mass

[23] For an especially cogent analysis of status politics see Joseph R. Gusfield, *Symbolic Crusade: Status Politics and the American Temperance Movement* (Urbana, Ill., 1963). The authors and articles cited in footnote 21 also discuss the topic.

action on political issues are much harder to find than examples of quiescence. We routinely institutionalize our symbolic reassurances in the form of constitutional or statutory guarantees and in the creation of administrative organizations. This contrasts with those political systems, such as the Latin American ones, in which the individual political figure or coterie pose as protectors. In the latter systems both the apparent absence of institutional protections and the vulnerability of the political leaders encourage extralegal collective action: vigilante movements and the coup d'etat.

CHAPTER 9

Mass Responses
to Political Symbols

I

In examining the acts, leadership styles, settings, and speeches that engage the attention of the spectators of politics the previous chapters of this book have foreshadowed some propositions about mass responses to the political scene. The basic thesis is that mass publics respond to currently conspicuous political symbols: not to "facts," and not to moral codes embedded in the character or soul, but to the gestures and speeches that make up the drama of the state.

The mass public does not study and analyze detailed data about secondary boycotts, provisions for stock ownership and control in a proposed space communications corporation, or missile installations in Cuba.[1] It ignores these things until political actions and speeches make them symbolically threatening or reassuring, and it then responds to the cues furnished by the actions and the speeches, not to direct knowledge of the facts.

It is therefore political actions that chiefly shape men's political wants and "knowledge," not the other way around. The common assumption that what democratic government does is somehow always a response to the moral codes, desires, and knowledge embedded inside people is as inverted as it is

[1] Campbell, Converse, Miller, and Stokes, *op. cit.*, p. 249.

reassuring. This model, avidly taught and ritualistically repeated, cannot explain what happens; but it may persist in our folklore because it so effectively sanctifies prevailing policies and permits us to avoid worrying about them.

Values, it is true, are persistent in the sense specified in the last chapter. Fundamental norms as created by reference groups persist, leading interested groups to claim increasing increments of the values the norms embody. How fast successive levels of benefit are sought or how intensely deprivations are resisted hinges upon what is legitimized and upon what is made to appear possible. Political acts and settings, leadership, and language all influence legitimations and assumptions about possibility.

A reversal in mass political demands respecting American policy toward Germany occurred, for example, in the years immediately following World War II. At the end of the war there were widespread demands for stamping out religious persecution, genocide, and dictatorship, and for eliminating those who had been associated with these German practices. The Nuremberg trials reflected this political configuration. A series of governmental actions rather swiftly replaced the assumption that the threat to be guarded against was Hitlerism, however, and replaced it with equally widespread fears of Russia. These actions included the creation of a new military alliance in NATO, jousting with Russia in the United Nations and elsewhere, and a series of other American and Russian acts dramatizing the emergence of a cold war, an iron curtain, and other symbols of a major new threat. The political acts to which the mass public responded may have been rational and effective or they may not. That question remains controversial and also irrelevant to this inquiry. That the response of spectators was to these acts, however, and not directly to exhaustive and dispassionate analysis of the military situation is central. The public is not in touch with the situation, and it "knows" the situation only through the symbols that engage it.

In view of the changed perceptual world created by the

symbols of cold war, "Germany" quickly took on a new meaning. There were new sources of anxiety and a new view of the future and the possible. Germany became an ally against Russia; and if former Nazis in high military and political posts could help cope with the new dangers, they were welcomed and their past actions rewritten or ignored. It thus turned out that very intense mass concerns about de- nazification were not generators of public policy, but rather highly vulnerable victims of a changed perceptual world.

It is clear enough that whatever promises and hazards men see as possibilities on the political horizon depend upon the assumptions created for them by political acts and events. The possibilities they perceive influence their immediate political demands and actions in turn.

Changes in mass response of the kind just illustrated are, of course, neither instantaneous nor unanimous. They entail struggle and resistance among people with different interests. By the same token they involve struggle and resistance within a great many ambivalent individuals who experience a some- times painful effort to find a new perceptual outlook that has more meaning than the one they have reason to abandon: a world that permits them to understand and to act with less tension. The political symbols that bring about the change do so, in one sense, by changing the tensions associated with the old and the new as they suggest altered possibilities.

II

Under what conditions are such changes in mass behavior likely and when will they be resisted? Because the factors involved are so closely dependent on each other, there is a danger that any analysis will distort by implying with undue certainty that some one social phenomenon is a cause or an independent variable. Let it be emphasized that we are deal- ing here with a total transaction. The theory that follows consists of a series of assumptions and inferences. Although we do not have adequate empirical observations to validate the entire theory, various segments are substantiated by findings in disparate fields of social science.

The degree of consensus or division in a society on issues that persist and arouse men emotionally is a useful starting point for the analysis of mass responses. Examples of such issues in the United States are: the status of minority religious, racial, and ethnic groups, restrictions on the economic activities of the wealthy, and willingness to compromise differences with other countries.

Mass responses depend upon whether public values with respect to strong norms of this kind are heavily concentrated (unimodal), polarized into two clearly defined adversary foci (bimodal), or dispersed rather widely along a scale (multimodal). The dispersion of values on one issue will often correspond in some measure with the dispersion on the other strong ones. In the United States, for example, people who oppose restrictions on economic activity may also be more likely than "welfare staters" to support racial, ethnic, or religious status distinctions and to be opposed to a "soft" line toward the Communist bloc. To the extent that such overlap exists, deep-seated cleavage or consensus is reinforced.

When, on the issues that arouse men emotionally, there is a bimodal value structuring, threat and insecurity are maximized. Those who hold the other value become the enemy. Under these circumstances condensation symbolism and mental rigidity become key factors in social interaction for reasons already considered, and it becomes relatively easy to shift men's assumptions about the future and therefore their responses to present conditions. Under this kind of value patterning, mass responses are more manipulable than under either of the other two to be considered because responses are chiefly to threat perceptions and can be readily changed by making it appear that new threats are now dominant.[2] George Orwell dramatized the possibilities in his novel *1984* with accounts of overnight changes in the na-

[2] Adorno and others, *op. cit.*, p. 661.

tional enemy and in history books: reversals enthusiastically accepted by the public.

A multimodal scattering of values is the opposite extreme. In this situation a very large part of the population is likely to see some merit in both sides of the argument: to be ambivalent and at the same time free to explore the possibilities of alternative courses of action. Rather than fear of an enemy, there is stimulating tension. A minimal fraction of the population is frozen in a narrow class or other fixed grouping, and a major fraction is marginal and searching for a synthesis.[3] Value structuring is therefore relatively slight. Rather than a fixed past and future, accepted with passion and carrying clear implications for present behavior, alternative possibilities can be recognized and pluralistic politics supported. The preconditions exist for cognitive planning, negotiation, and logrolling.

The unimodal value structure is the type to which the American population has most closely conformed through most of United States history. Here there is a wide measure of consensus on the fundamental policy directions of the state. In this kind of polity nongovernmental groups and organizations enjoy a maximum degree of maneuverability because they are not constantly opposed by adversary groupings, and most of the public remains uninvolved and uncritical.

At the same time the unimodal structure encourages a maximum of democratic procedures, forms, and structuring because political parties and private power groups will predictably move in the same direction. There can be open and dramatic appeals for public support, for the support is already great and the likelihood of massive opposition to basic policies slight. The creation and dramatic employment of democratic forms may therefore be not so much an indication of responsiveness to changing popular values as a sign that values are unimodal and that the mass public is uncritical. In a unimodal situation evocative political symbols are

[3] See the quote from Karl Mannheim, p. 89.

likely to have similar meanings and call forth similar responses in a larger proportion of the population than under
other conditions. This result is likely because the people are
more alike in respect to education, socioeconomic status, up-
bringing, experiences, and ambitions.

There is good reason to suspect that wide agreement on a
centrist or "middle of the road" orientation offers a barrier
to politically induced change. Nongovernmental organizations then become the foci of change in tangible resource allocations. There is a built-in depreciation of tension and
criticism, so that responsiveness to suggestions for innovation is slight, leading to low viability, to great suspicion of
critics of the status quo, and eventually to mass movements
dedicated not to change but to the suppression of heretics.
In this respect Aristotle's contention that popular government gives way eventually to tyranny jibes in some degree
with the view of recent mass society theorists, such as Kornhauser, who believe they can record a movement from plur-
alism to mass society.[4]

Tension levels play a key role in this theory. It suggests
that a bimodal value structure creates such great tension that
rational responses are held to a minimum and symbolic cues
and assurances avidly grasped. A unimodal structure creates
little tension regarding norms, leaving a clear field for organized group maneuvering but also creating the conditions
for the emergence of mass society symptoms if deviants or
"outsiders" appear to be threatening the consensus. A multimodal structure comes closest to establishing optimal tension for critical mass response to policy proposals. Harold
Lasswell observed three decades ago that "the dynamic of
politics is to be found in the tension level of the individuals
in society."[5]

Clearly the model deals with ideal types. A polity that is
basically unimodal, for example, may become bimodal on a
major issue for a period of years and begin to exhibit the

[4] Kornhauser, *op. cit.*
[5] Lasswell, *Psychopathology and Politics*, p. 185.

characteristics of the latter form. Though pure examples of any type may be hard to find in the real world, this theory predicts what kinds of mass response are likely for a particular patterning of values.

The political party structure of a country offers a clue to the dispersal of fundamental values among its population. Anthony Downs has developed an "economic theory of democracy," which suggests, among other things, that a unimodal value structure gives rise to a two party system and a bimodal or multimodal structure to a multiple party system.[6] In Italy and France, where popular values are more clearly bimodal than in other democracies, in the Scandinavian countries, which conform most closely to the multimodal type, and in the United States his proposition fits well. The Downs theory would also lead one to expect the current trend toward a two party system in West Germany.

III

The constant involvement of private organizations and groups in actions that are essentially public in character has been a major theme of this discussion. We turn now to another sense in which private groups and public institutions are integrally related.

Man is constantly creating and responding to symbols, whether he is at any moment concerned with public affairs or not. Susanne Langer declares:

This basic need, which certainly is obvious only in man, is the need of symbolization. The symbol-making function is one of man's primary activities, like eating, looking, or moving about. It is the fundamental process of his mind, and goes on all the time.

. . . . .

The material furnished by the senses is constantly wrought into symbols, which are our elementary ideas. Some of these ideas can

[6] Anthony Downs, *An Economic Theory of Democracy* (New York, 1957).

be combined and manipulated in the manner we call "reasoning." Others do not lend themselves to this use, but are naturally telescoped into dreams, or vapor off in conscious fantasy; and a vast number of them build the most typical and fundamental edifice of the human mind — religion.[7]

While men differ in the meanings symbols convey to them and in the manner of their reaction, no man can remain alive and avoid symbolic response. As has already been suggested, following Mead, this is what gives him a self and a mind.

Symbolic involvement with governmental acts, settings, and actors can therefore be recognized as one of various devices by which men engage themselves in a fashion that is symbolically necessary and satisfying. Religion, as Langer points out, is another such universal device, and work, together with the economic organizations in which it involves men, is a third major one. Family attachments and participation in social organizations also contribute to the richness or emptiness of man's symbolic life.

There is reason to believe that the style of men's symbolic engagements in these various associations is related and often contagious, and that they are sometimes complementary in the sense that needs not supplied by one of them may be sought in another. Generalizations must remain tentative.

Certainly a central dimension of involvement in all of them lies between the poles of identification and alienation. A great many people, particularly specialists, professionals, and managers in industry, develop a tie to their work that is relatively rational and efficient. Their effectiveness derives from their special ability to devise methods of accomplishing desired ends, and they experience deep satisfaction as they exercise such ability. As suggested earlier, such rational and effective manipulation of resources is in part a function of the opportunity to work with the concrete environment and to see the results of one's work. Nobody functions in this way

[7] Langer, *Philosophy in a New Key*, pp. 32–33.

in everything he does, and some people apparently never do so. It may be that only people who have learned through some such gratifying association how to deal effectively with men and objects are likely to respond to political leadership and movements in a way that serves their objective interests and brings them tangible resources. There is evidence in earlier chapters that business management and other organized elites are consistently most effective in gaining resources through government. This is not to say that most individual managers or specialists are effective at political tactics or even that they are directly involved, for survey research indicates that, "political participation to satisfy economic needs is unrelated to level of income in the American culture." [8] The consistent success of organized elites in utilizing the governmental process to serve their material interests does suggest, however, both that some individual managers and specialists are effective at it and that their constituents have learned how to support them and how to avoid defeating their efforts through irrational actions.

People who are effective in some of their activities may nonetheless seek nonrational satisfactions from other pursuits. The highly effective specialist or manager may identify with his company or his profession in an emotional manner. His opinions on political matters unrelated to his economic interests may serve chiefly to project inner tensions or to aid in social adjustment. As an extreme example, Henry Ford, who epitomized rationality in organizing the production of automobiles, became transfixed with undemonstrable and unreal threats and distortions when behaving in other settings.

Ford was extreme, not typical. For most men who function well and effectively, condensation symbols evidently serve as a spur, catalyst, and complement to their work. If they are sure, without objective evidence, that what is good for General Motors is good for the country, the belief doubtless makes them work with greater zeal for General Motors,

[8] Lane, *op. cit.*, p. 107.

and the sense of harmony both their work and their beliefs confer may also make them work more effectively for their country if called to do so. The testing of work and its results remains a testing against tangible results, not satisfaction with pipedreams.

Similarly, effective workmanship in a man's occupation frequently occurs together with a high degree of identification with condensation symbols in his religious life, the two activities apparently complementing and enriching each other by reinforcing a feeling of usefulness and of being an important part of something larger than oneself. The key contrast in man's symbolic engagements with work, state, church, and other associations is not the difference between identification and hostility, but that between satisfying involvement and despairing noninvolvement.

For those whose identification with work, political party, and community is slight and unsatisfying, the yearning to escape from isolation and responsibility becomes very strong. The alienated man, who feels little sense of belonging to any group and cherishes no organization as an extension of his own personality, will, for reasons already explored, predictably become authoritarian. He will seek strong leadership, personalize, stereotype and distort his environment, and will react to distortions and abstractions rather than to concrete people and things.

Lipset has called attention to the prevalence of "working class authoritarianism." [9] Among unskilled workers ethnocentric and authoritarian reactions are apparently more common than among those with higher socioeconomic status. This condition is understandable as in part at least a resultant of the working conditions for unskilled labor in modern industry. Summing up the environmental influences contributing to mass authoritarian movements Frenkel-Brunswik has written: "In our society the increasing mental standardization accompanying the processes of mass production, the increasing difficulty of genuine identification with soci-

[9] S. M. Lipset, *Political Man* (New York, 1960), pp. 97–130.

ety due to the anonymity of the big organizations and the ensuing isolation of the individual, the unintelligibility of political and social forces, the decline of the individual's ability to decide and master his life rationally and autonomously, and finally the power of propaganda machinery to manipulate — are among the most potent of the factors which might contribute to such mass support in the foreseeable future." [10]

To divide work in the factory to the point that the worker cannot have any feeling of satisfaction, accomplishment, or autonomy is to emphasize to the worker throughout the day that he is being used as a machine and not as a man. Here is one facet of modern social organization that has clear implications for obsessive symbol seeking in the political and religious realms.

In addition, as Lipset points out, working-class family life is usually more authoritarian and offers fewer affective attachments than is true of the middle classes, and working class people are less often involved in community organizations. Here is a fairly clear tie between the quality of political participation and the character of private life.

There is reason to suspect that for some people or under some conditions politics and religion serve as alternatives to each other as symbol suppliers. People may rely chiefly on one or the other to satisfy a need to belong and to believe. The Western tradition of conflict between church and state doubtless has depended partly on the realization that such competition occurs. The antichurch policies of modern totalitarian states and the acceptance of a political ideology or a state as sacred by masses under stress also reflects it. A recent study in the United States may suggest one form this phenomenon takes in a democratic polity. The following table presents responses at various dates to the question, "Which one of these groups do you feel is doing the most good for the country at the present time?" [11]

[10] Frenkel-Brunswik, *op. cit.*, p. 378.
[11] Adapted from *Opinion News*, Sept. 15, 1947, p. 12, in Wendell Bell,

Type of Leader	Sept., 1942	Dec., 1943	June, 1946	June, 1947
			(percentages)	
Religious leaders	17	26	32	33
Business leaders	19	17	18	19
Government leaders	28	24	13	15
Labor leaders	6	7	10	11
Congress	6	10	7	7
Undecided	24	11	21	18

Notice that while the percentage of people who admired business leaders or Congress or were undecided changed very little over the years, favorable response to religious leaders increased in almost exactly the same proportion that favorable response to government leaders declined; and the change in both was very great over a five-year period.

If satisfying involvement in work and in religion has these implications for political engagement, some current trends in industry and in the churches are relevant to the quality of men's political responses. The great bulk of jobs in industry, unskilled and semiskilled, offer little scope to exercise an "instinct of workmanship," and therefore slight basis for gratification through work. It is not yet clear what difference more automation will make. An increasing proportion of white collar jobs is not necessarily a trend toward the "human use of human beings." The growing importance of specialists in organizations may be such a trend, though Thompson has pointed out that organizational myths and rites have so far been remarkably successful in concealing the widening divergence between ability and formal authority in large organizations.[12]

Though church membership and attendance have reached new highs since World War II, even the most cursory exam-

Richard J. Hill, and Charles B. Wright, *Public Leadership* (San Francisco, 1961), p. 143.

[12] Thompson, *op. cit.*

ination of the quality of attachment to churches suggests that the increase represents largely a groping of the alienated for some kind of attachment rather than a gratifying involvement with religion. To attend church may be to signal one's anxiety about looking like a nonconforming agnostic; and to respond to the religiosity sometimes found there is to signal one's divorcement from religion.

The political realm, unlike work and church, is always available for evocative use as masses need to use it. There is no tie to a manifestly trivial and mechanical function as in unskilled work, but rather the assurance that each voter's part is significant. Nor is there a setting calling for a competitive display of clothes, conformity, and sentimentality, as in many churches, but rather a sense of belonging to something real and decisive. Politics can therefore become a residual supplier of the symbols that men require.

A number of students influenced by Freud have observed that an increase in demand for political acts that gratify sensuality accompanies widespread alienation or loss of faith in the rationality of social processes. One way to fight anomie is to fall back upon the excitement of the senses. This sometimes takes the form of libidinous attachment to leaders. It also typically takes the form of puritanism, with its accompanying sadism and masochism, including the suppression of books, art, theater, and political dissent.

A parallel mass response has been noticed by students approaching the subject from various vantage points. Bruno Bettelheim is representative of a group of psychologists who have emphasized the disposition of the dispossessed and the deprived to accept the values and assumptions of their exploiters, for only through such behavior can the dispossessed be recognized as individuals and as a legitimate part of a larger system.[13] Charles Morris' analysis of "pathic language," facilitating the same result, has already been mentioned.[14] Kenneth Burke makes the point in the following way: "even

[13] Bettelheim, *op. cit.*
[14] See Chapter 6.

the dispossessed tends to feel that he "has a stake in" the authoritative structure that dispossesses him; for the influence exerted upon the policies of education by the authoritative structure encourages the dispossessed to feel that his only hope of repossession lies in his allegiance to this structure that has dispossessed him. . . . If he would get a job or better the job he has, he must win the good favor of those in authority." [15]

IV

One of George Herbert Mead's greatest insights was his discovery that through a "conversation of gestures" man creates his own world. How people act, which symbols become significant and what they signify, and what there is for men to act upon are not hard "givens," but are created for individual selves through role-taking.

A natural assumption is that men see political events and institutions and then react to what they see, explaining their reasons for doing so. Careful observation reveals, however, that a "given" world is a fiction. Men perceive and only then see. In one respect after another it appears that the vantage point for perception becomes a key to mass behavior.

Illustrations of this phenomenon are easy to cite, and their implications for political behavior are important. Do men, for example, look with innocent eyes at the activities of Barry Goldwater, objectively judge them, and then act accordingly? If the psychological process of perception were that simple, perceptions would obviously be far more consistent than they observably are. We would not have a large group of the population consistently perceiving Goldwater's actions as taking one form and another group consistently perceiving the same actions as taking the opposite form. We are constantly aware of the strong effort, often conscious but more significantly subconscious, of supporters and of opponents of a political figure to see what they want to see: to

[15] Burke, *Attitudes Toward History*, p. 232.

make the world conform to the pattern that fits their conceptual framework and values. Observation of politics is not simply an effort to learn what is happening but rather a process of making observations conform to assumptions.

The student of political process therefore makes a serious mistake if he takes political perceptions and verbal justifications of political attitudes as fixed entities that predict future behavior and attitudes. They will do so only as long as the respondents continue to respond to the same symbols through taking the same roles. Perception of political events and rationalizations of political attitudes are to be understood not as independent variables or as causes of behavior, but rather as signals of a particular kind of role taking and symbolization. Only when they are studied as such signals do they become clues to political dynamics.

Only then, for example, does it become clear that a succession of conspicuous events in the news is routinely perceived by a group as having a particular metaphorical meaning, no matter what the events may be, while the same series of events may have a quite different meaning for a group reacting to different symbols. For one group a Khrushchev ultimatum on Berlin is a necessary reaction to American war mongering and his later withdrawal of the ultimatum is confirmation of his ambition for peace. To another group the ultimatum "proves" the assumption that Khrushchev is intent on creating a casus belli, while his withdrawal is perceived as a tactical ploy, evidence of his shiftiness and aggressive intent.

Fed by such "evidence," the metaphor grows more vivid and compelling unless a radical realignment of roles occurs. Hence the pervasive perception of deepening crisis in public affairs. Himmelstrand demonstrated this effect experimentally, concluding that: "An increase in expressive concern manifests itself in an increased *intensity* of activities in some restricted sub-area of symbolic activity rather than in the *extension* of the action family." [16]

[16] Himmelstrand, *op. cit.*, p. 267.

A central aspect of the metaphoric political world into which perceptions are fitted is a mythic time dimension. Selective creation of a past and a future justifies contemporary interests. Dwelling on the past or the future in either millenial or threatening terms may be taken as a signal of present anxiety, and the character of the utopia that is created specifies the respects in which present threat is perceived. An anxious and antibusiness public of the 1930's responds sympathetically to the depiction of the business moguls of the late nineteenth century as unscrupulous robber barons; and a public that takes the business role in the 1950's welcomes a new set of histories depicting the same tycoons as men who made a "creative response" to their times. The Luce publications and a sympathetic section of the public legitimize a mammoth defense establishment and a series of military alliances by creating a future in the form of "The American Century." Man cannot live with himself, with his state, or with his state of affairs unless he continuously re-creates his past, his present, and his future in the light of his significant symbols. In the measure that socialization processes and reference groups are alike, groups of people create their worlds in a common image and develop common political interests.

Conclusion

Once the forms of symbolic interplay in politics are specified and their political functions examined, it becomes clear that some common social psychological mechanisms tie them together. Role-taking is one central theme, especially powerful in influencing the behaviors of public officials and political leaders. A continuing tension between threat and reassurance is another central theme, explaining the reactions of general publics to political symbols. A review of the functions of these two mechanisms accordingly serves to summarize the major propositions of this book and to help place them in perspective.

Through taking the roles of publics whose support they need, public officials achieve and maintain their positions of leadership. The official who correctly gauges the response of publics to his acts, speeches, and gestures makes those behaviors significant symbols, evoking common meanings for his audience and for himself and so shaping his further actions as to reassure his public and in this sense "represent" them.

One type of group whose roles officials must share are the organized interests whose activities law purports to regulate. Thus, regulatory agency officials, through mutual role-sharing with the regulated, typically act so as to facilitate a high measure of evasion of the formal rules. Role-taking within the agency's staff, amounting to institutional pressures for conformity, contributes to this same result. The evasions or lax law enforcement are further facilitated by ambiguous legal and administrative language and by bargaining in which the regulated can exert sanctions against public officials, directly or indirectly. The official's acts thus reassure these organized groups and win them tangible benefits in line with their bargaining power. Administrative acts become symbols both of protection of a wide public and of the ability of regulators to see issues from the point of view of the regulated. Tension between threat and reassurance inevitably continues for all concerned; but role-taking assures that a viable pattern of private and public action will emerge: that both private and public actors will survive and that the former can continue to exert what sanctions they possess. This last result occurs as a function of the unpublicized part of the decision-making process: the bargaining and the acceptance of evasions.

At the same time the more widely known facets of this same process reassure large publics who view the political scene as spectators and who lack direct bargaining sanctions. These people perceive threats of a different sort: those that come from a sense of ineffectiveness in the face of ominous news developments in a world they are constantly told about but cannot touch, and the threats that flow from their own inner tensions.

For these spectators of politics the more dramatic and publicized features of the political process convey reassurance, but they can do so only because people are ambivalent and anxious for reassurance. Hortatory speeches justify regulatory programs as protecting widespread public interests. Legal language commands enforcement of the same protections in terms that look precise to the laymen even though they look ambiguous to the professional lawyer or student of political science. Judicial and administrative hearings maintain the forms of rational weighing of evidence and of the interests of wide publics even while they make it easy for administrators, judges, and juries to take the roles both of the violators and of the injured. The acting out in formal, adversary hearings of the ambivalence that springs from men's conflicting interests and perceptions legitimizes the decisions flowing from these dramatic forms.

Many other highly valued and widely publicized political institutions further help legitimize policies and contribute to public support for them. Voting may be the most fundamental of all devices for reassuring masses that they are participants in the making of public policy. The political leader's gestures dramatizing his ability to cope with the threats the public fears win him the following he needs. Men's anxious search for direction in a world many of them find alien encourage them to accept such gestures of leadership as valid and effective, particularly as it is rarely possible to trace the leader's acts to their consequences. In place of impersonal threatening forces, followers are reassured by a dramaturgy of personal coping, even if it is not demonstrable that the leader shares their values or brings them to realization in concrete benefits.

The settings of formal political acts help "prove" the integrity and legitimacy of the acts they frame, creating a semblance of reality from which counterevidence is excluded. Settings also help leaders find the roles and identifications that are significant to followers.

Language forms and terms reinforce the reassuring perspectives established through other political symbols, subtly interweaving with action to help shape values, norms, and assumptions about future possibilities. Abstractions like democracy and justice are reified and identified with existing political institutions. The structure of "socially pathic" language encourages attachments to the very institutions which deny men values they prize. Potential opposition to group claims is forestalled through the stretching of the meaning of symbols to make them conform to what is required of people bureaucratically or physically. Trite phrases may be used as incantations, serving to dull the critical faculties.

The fundamentally insatiable character of political goals also contributes to the constant tension between arousal and reassurance in political spectators. The names of political goals, being logical categories rather than signs of concrete needs, cannot be satisfied through concrete benefits. Such benefits simply increase aspiration levels. Quiescence occurs only as periodically renewed political acts and gestures in support of groups with particular goals come to symbolize the backing of the state for the groups concerned. Such acts become symbols of status.

Divisions among groups on the policy issues that arouse men most keenly and run most widely through society are a major source of tension and of the need for reassurance, and the extent of such divisions accordingly helps determine the potency of political symbols and receptivity to them. Where people's jobs or church activities underline their alienation rather than promoting satisfying ties to others, the need for symbolic reassurance through politics becomes all the greater.

In all these ways, the role-taking of public officials and the psychic tensions and ambivalences of onlookers contribute to the symbolic potency of political acts, leadership styles, settings, and language.

The themes a society emphasizes and re-emphasizes about its government may not accurately describe its politics; but they do at least tell us what men want to believe about themselves and their state. In some cultures men have chosen to believe that their rulers were gods or descendants of gods; or that they were divinely appointed to rule. Men have sometimes told themselves that the established machinery for selecting leaders and legislators necessarily produced rule by an able aristocracy, or rule in the interest of a chosen class: the proletariat, the warriors, or the large landholders. Often men have told themselves that their political institutions translate the will of the mass of the people into public policies.

In some metaphysical sense all these propositions may be true; but it is of more interest to the social scientist that they are often not demonstrable by scientific methods, that there are many exceptions to them, and that they continue to be believed in spite of the lack of evidence and of the demonstrable exceptions. Clearly, beliefs like these serve functions other than the description of a country's political institutions. They help hold men together and help maintain an orderly state.

In the United States it is easy enough to identify the propositions we emphasize and re-emphasize about our government: in the teaching of children, in political oratory, in popular writing and common talk, and, above all, in the citing of shocking "exceptions" to the way the government should operate.

We tell ourselves that the people determine what government will do, and we point to elections, legislative actions, and "soundings" of the public as evidence.

We believe that our machinery of government functions so that administrators carry out the will of the legislature, and therefore of the people, rather than making policy by themselves. Our laws require them to do so and establish penalties for administrative actions that are not sanctioned by law.

We assure ourselves that a government that satisfies public demands thereby wins popular support; that is, that public issues are important in the choice of executives and legislators and that satisfying particular demands brings political contentment. This belief is basic to our faith in popular sovereignty.

Finally, we tell ourselves that government has the power and knowledge to produce the results the people want. Political candidates promise results, and we praise or blame leaders according to how well affairs have gone: economically, militarily, diplomatically, and so on.

That the departures from these assumptions are not exceptions but quite routine is evident from a great deal of political science research, some of it cited in this book. It sums up the larger themes of the book to suggest an alternative set of propositions about American government: propositions that account for the frequency of the "exceptions" and that help explain what observably happens rather than what we wish would happen.

(1) What people get from government is what administrators do about their problems rather than the promises of statutes, constitutions, or oratory. Administrators have wide leeway in practice to respond to the interests of groups that can exert economic, political, moral, or organizational sanctions against them. In doing so they are not "selling out"; they are simply taking the roles their organizational positions make them recognize as viable.

(2) The assumption by the mass public that what administrators do is ordained by a legislative and public "will" sanctifies administrative actions and helps make them acceptable.

(3) It can rarely be known what concrete future effects public laws and acts will bring. Economic interactions, psychological responses, the actions of foreign governments and of domestic groupings all contribute to uncertainty. Because men are anxious about impersonal, uncontrollable, or unknowable events, however, they constantly substitute personality for impersonality in interpreting political events. They attribute wider maneuverability to leaders than the latter enjoy. They want to believe that officials have the power and knowledge to produce particular results. They give their allegiance most wholeheartedly to the chief executive whose gestures proclaim that he can deal with the enemy, quite apart from concrete results.

(4) The achievement of a political goal by an interested group leads to claims for more of the same kind of benefit and not to contentment. Only through symbolic reassurance that "the state" recognizes the claims and status of the group as legitimate is quiescence brought about, and the reassurance must be periodically renewed.

(5) It is through speeches, gestures, and settings that evoke reassuring anticipations that men's political claims are limited and public order maintained. Political talk, back-

grounds, and poses are commonplace and ordinarily not analyzed. For that very reason their covert implications engage us all the more subtly and powerfully.

These propositions lead us to expect quite different kinds of behavior from officials, organized groups, and the general public from those described in the formal and popular accounts of how government works. They may not erase our disappointment at the "exceptions" to the latter, but they do erase our surprise.

INDEX

The Symbolic Uses of Politics

Ritual, defined, 16; 3, 4, 17, 47, 57, 58, 60
Rokeach, Milton, 31n, 48
Role-taking, 44–45, 49–51, 53, 57, 71, 111, 188–194. *See also* Dramaturgy; Political drama
Role theory, 69–72, 84
Roosevelt, Franklin D., 78, 80, 82, 83, 94, 100, 108
Roosevelt, Theodore, 94
Ross, Arthur M., 34n

Sacco-Vanzetti case, 70
Saenger, Gerhart, 31n
Salomon, Albert, 32, 33n
Sapir, Edward, 6n, 116n, 120, 121n, 131n, 159, 160n
Saporta, Sol, 120n
Sarnoff, I., 35n
Satisfaction, 127, 179–180
Schachter, Stanley, 32n, 35n
Schiller, Friedrich, 11
Sears, Pauline S., 162n
Second-class mail, 65
Securities Exchange Commission, 41
Securities exchange legislation, 41
Self-reinforcement. *See* Reassurance
Settings, political. *See* Political settings
Sheatsley, Paul B., 81
Sherif, Muzafer, 53n, 86, 108
Sherman Act, 26
Shils, Edward A., 90n, 166n
Silver purchase provisions, 27, 28
Simon, Herbert A., 34n, 44n, 49, 50, 51, 54, 55, 68, 112n, 145n
Smith, M. Brewster, 7, 164
Smith Act, 70
Smithburg, Donald W., 44n
Social adjustment, 8, 180
Social images. *See* Identification; Perception
Social movements, 89–90, 167–171
Social security, 42
Social Security Act, 154

Sociological theory, 10, 34–35, 167, 170
State services, 83
Status, 170
Steffens, Lincoln, 51
Steiner, Gilbert Y., 60n, 136, 147n
Stevenson, Adlai, 7, 131
Stewart, Irwin, 72
Stogdill, Ralph M., 53n, 54n
Stokes, Donald E., 3n, 138n, 156n, 172n
Storing, Herbert J., 50, 55
Stouffer, Samuel A., 155n, 161n
Strauss, Anselm L., 34, 35n, 103n, 131n, 142n
Style, 132–133, 190; administrative, 142–145; bargaining, 145–149; elements of, 132–133; hortative, 134–138; legal, 138–142
Suci, George, 30n
Sullivan, Denis, 162n
Sullivan, Harry Stack, 81n, 85
Supreme Court, 12, 81, 90, 108
Survey Research Center, 156
Symbiosis, 58–60, 66, 68
Symbols. *See* Condensation symbols; Referential symbols
Syntax, 126. *See also* Cues

Taft, William Howard, 83
Taft-Hartley Act, 26, 27, 53, 67, 68, 141
Tannenbaum, Percy, 30n
Tennessee Valley Authority, 52
Theory. *See* Administrative theory; Anthropological theory; Organization theory; Political theory; Psychological theory; Role theory; Sociological theory
Thomas, Norman, 131
Thompson, Victor A., 44n, 45, 46n, 54n, 75n, 79n, 183
Threats, 13–14, 47, 49, 69, 70, 188–189
Till, Irene, 24n
Tolman, E. C., 166n
Truman, David, 24, 27, 39n, 55n, 145n

Index

United Nations, 173
USSR, 15

Vaihinger, Hans, 119
Values, 4, 50, 52, 85, 107, 120, 125, 146, 155, 165–166, 173, 175–178
Veblen, Thorstein, 9
Vigilantism, 167–168
Voting behavior, 2–3, 27–28, 30, 43, 122–123, 138

Wage Stabilization Board, 55

Wahl, C. W., 3n, 19n, 110n
War Labor Board, 55
Warner, W. Lloyd, 106, 107n
Weber, Max, 77, 117, 118, 129
Welch, Robert, 131
White, R. W., 7, 164
Whitehead, Donald F., 70n
Whitney, Richard, 41
Whorf, Benjamin L., 120n
Whyte, William Foote, 86
Wilcox, Clair, 24n, 39n, 65n
Wright, Charles B., 183n